WINTER DAY PLAY!

WINTER DAY PLAY!

Activities, Crafts, and Games
for Indoors and Out

Nancy F. Castaldo

CHICAGO
REVIEW
PRESS

Library of Congress Cataloging-in-Publication Data

Is available from the Library of Congress.

Cover design and illustration: Fran Lee
Interior design and illustration: Rattray Design

First edition
Published by Chicago Review Press, Incorporated
814 North Franklin Street
Chicago, Illinois 60610
ISBN 1-55652-381-5
Printed in the United States of America

5 4 3 2 1

For my godson, John Deere, with love.

Always for Lucie.

CONTENTS

ACKNOWLEDGMENTS

A special thanks to my family and friends, who
are always there through the long winters.
Thanks also to the members of my Girl Scout
troop, who inspire me and who are always
willing to try something new.

INTRODUCTION

THAT FIRST WINTER snowfall is such an exciting time. We rush out, eager to feel the soft, cold snowflakes that sparkle on our hair and light on our noses. We reach out our tongues in hopes of a taste. The first snowfall is often light, just a dusting, giving us a hint of things to come. Then, after a couple of those dustings, we finally have the big one. It's a snow day! Everything stops and it's time to pull on your boots and mittens and have some real snowy fun.

Winter Day Play! was written for all of those days—those without snow, those with a hint of snow, and the big ones. There are activities that will help children discover the magic of snowflakes, learn new games, and experience the winter holidays of other cultures. Most activities are perfect for one child or a whole classroom. Most of all, *Winter Day Play!* will help keep that excitement of the first snowfall throughout the whole winter, with activities, crafts, and games that will inspire, encourage, and release the creativity of each child.

Note: The symbol ❄ indicates that assistance from a grown-up is needed.

WINTER DAY PLAY!

INTO THE SNOW

Fun is waiting in the snow,

So turn the page and there you go.

1

SNOW CASTLES

I or more kids

Have you ever sat on a beach and made a sand castle? A snow castle is just as much fun to create and you don't have to worry about a wave washing it away.

WHAT YOU NEED

Snow

Sand shovel and pail

Plastic food storage containers

Sand toys

Paper cups

What You Do

1. Experiment with your building supplies. Using your shovel and pail, fill each of your sand toys and containers with snow and pack down the snow with your hand. (Make sure to wear mittens!) Turn the containers over and gently tap the bottom for the snow to come out. Take a look at all the different shapes. Which ones will you use for your castle?

2. You will need a flat surface of snow to build your castle. Stomp down some snow or ask a grown-up to flatten an area with a snow shovel.

3. Begin filling up the containers that you will use for the base of your castle. Which shapes should you start with, the bigger shapes or the smaller shapes? Try them both. Is your castle going to be round or square? Think about what you want your

finished castle to look like as you build the base. When you have a design in mind, in the cleared space turn the containers over and gently tap the bottom of each.

4. Add your other shapes to the castle. Does your castle have a tower, a moat, or a wall? Paper cups work great for towers.

5. Decorate your castle. Use items from around your yard. Evergreen branches make great trees. What else can you use to decorate? When you are finished, take out your action figures or dolls and pretend they live in an enchanted world of ice and snow. When you're finished playing, remember to bring them in; otherwise you may not find your toys until the spring thaw!

MAKE A JAPANESE SNOW COTTAGE

I or more kids

Japanese children celebrate the Kamakura Festival in January by building snow cottages called "kamakuras." People in Japan have been celebrating the festival of Kamakura for about 200 years.

Part of the festival is to honor Suijin, the Japanese god of water. Children build an altar to the god of water in their kamakuras. They sit on a straw mat while wrapped in a warm quilt. Parents and friends visit them and are offered rice cakes and sweet rice drinks. In return, they leave fruit or coins for their hosts.

Here's how to make your own kamakura.

WHAT YOU NEED

A lot of snow

Shovel

Paper

Markers

❄ A grown-up to help

What You Do

1. Ask a grown-up to help you heap the snow into a large mound, about 5 feet (1.5 meters) high and about 4 (1.2 meters) to 5 feet (1.5 meters) wide.

2. Pack the mound firmly into the shape of a cylinder or igloo.

4

3. Start hollowing out the mound with the shovel or your hands to form a room. Remember to keep the sides thick enough so that your kamakura does not cave in.

4. Decorate your completed kamakura with poems or wishes written on sheets of paper, just as they do in Japan, and pressed into the outside walls. Place a mat or quilt on the floor to sit on and make yourself at home. Invite friends and family to visit you.

Kamakuras at Night

Children in Japan light their kamakuras with candles at night. Decorate your kamakura at night with your own luminaries. They are easy to create using small brown paper bags. Simply draw a star or other design on each bag. Use scissors to cut out the design. Set the bags in the snow. Place a flashlight inside each bag, or ask a grown-up to pour a bit of sand into each bag and place a votive candle inside the bag. Create a path to your kamakura with lighted luminaries. Invite friends and family to visit in the early evening after the sun has gone down. Your kamakura is a great place to enjoy the winter sky or listen for nearby owls.

SNOW PAINTING

I or more kids

Create a masterpiece with the snow as your canvas. Unlike your other pictures, it cannot hang on the refrigerator door—unless, of course, you remember to take a picture of it.

What You Do

1. Fill each of the spray bottles with water.

2. Add several drops of a different food coloring to each bottle to create your palette of color.

3. Head out into the snow with your color bottles. Squirt your bottles in a practice area of snow to see how much color sprays out. If the color is too light and difficult to see in the snow, you may want to add a few more drops of food coloring to the bottle to deepen your color.

4. When you are ready to paint, mark off a square in the snow with your stick to create your snow canvas.

5. Using your stick,
   draw your picture.
   Paint your picture using
   your spray bottles of color. Try
   painting a sledding race course, a
   crazy rainbow-colored snowman, or a
   large tic-tac-toe board on your lawn.
   Still need more ideas? Paint a message,
   a letter to Santa, or a garden of flowers.

ICY IGLOOS AND SASSY SCULPTURES

I or more kids

ver 200 years ago, chefs in France began to use ice sculptures to keep food cold during banquets. Since then, ice sculptures have graced the tables of many special dinners, but they have also found a place off the table. Winterfests all over the world boast spectacular sculptures created solely of ice. You might see huge swans, trains, castles, and even turtles made out of ice when you visit a winterfest. On a smaller scale, you can make your own ice sculpture that may last all winter if the weather stays cold enough.

WHAT YOU NEED

Plastic containers, all sizes and shapes

Ice cube tray

Water

Waterproof mittens

❄ A grown-up to help

What You Do

1. Fill the plastic containers with water and set them outside overnight to freeze, or put them in your freezer.

2. While the water is freezing, think about what you would like to create.

3. Check your containers. Are they all frozen? If so, collect them outside and turn them over carefully to free the ice from each container. If the ice won't come out of the container, tap the container gently on the ground. If you still have difficulty, dip the bottom in a bucket of warm water.

4. Look at the shapes you have created. Which ones will work with your design?

5. Build your design by stacking and combining the shapes that you have created. Cold water will help your shapes stick together. Drizzle a little water or snow on your ice to act like glue between the shapes you are stacking. Be sure to hold your pieces for a few moments to allow them time to adhere. If you are not happy with the outcome of your design, just pour a little warm water on the shapes to pry them apart and start over. Ask a grown-up to help you.

SNOW ANGELS

nyone can make a snow angel. You just lie down in the snow on your back and flap your arms and legs in the snow to form two half circles around your body. It's that easy. So, what else is there to do? Let's see.

Snow Angel Tips

1. Draw a halo above your angel's head with a stick.

2. Instead of the usual wings, create wings out of evergreen branches, fanned out from the body.

3. Color your angel with snow paint (page 6).

4. Experiment with different arm and leg positions to create snow kids instead of snow angels.

5. Have a snow angel decorating contest with your friends.

6. Play snow angel tag. See how many snow angels you can create before you get tagged.

7. Play ring around the rosy, but when you all fall down, make a circle of snow angels.

8. What other shapes can you make with your body while lying in the snow?

SUPER SNOWMEN

I or more kids

Have you ever made a snowman? If you haven't, they are easy and a lot of fun to make. So move over, Frosty, there're some new snow people outside this winter!

WHAT YOU NEED

Dense, packing snow

Scarf and other clothes to dress your snowman

Nuts, apples, charcoal, or other items to decorate the face of your snowman

What You Do

1. Start by making three large snowballs. Roll the snowballs in the snow to make them really big.

2. Stack the balls on top of each other, with the largest on the bottom. Now comes the fun part—decorating!

3. Is your snowman a boy or a girl? Does it wear a hat and a scarf? Is it a kid or a grown-up? Decorate and dress your snowman accordingly. Remember, carrots make great noses and branches make great arms. Use your imagination.

4. Write a poem, song, or story about your snowman.

Frosty the Snowman

Do you know the words to this famous holiday song about a snowman brought to life by a magic top hat? You probably do. What you probably don't know is that this song was originally sung by a famous cowboy/actor named Gene Autry back in 1950. It was written by Steve Nelson and Jack Rollins. In 1969 it was made into a holiday special for television and quickly became a holiday favorite. Now it's available on video, too. This year ask a grown-up to watch *Frosty the Snowman* with you.

THE BIG THAW EXPERIMENT

1 or more kids

Snow from the mountains melts during the spring thaw to fill rivers, lakes, and streams. We use the water for many things. Can you think of at least five?

Here's a fun experiment that will show you how much water can be found in melting snow.

What You Do

1. Fill the measuring cup with snow. Make sure you don't fill the cup beyond the top line. Can you read the measuring cup? How much snow did you collect? Write down the amount on your paper. Keep the snow in the cup.

2. Bring the measuring cup inside your kitchen. Ask a grown-up to help you with the next steps.

WHAT YOU NEED

Snow

Measuring cup

Paper

Pencil

Spoon

Pot

Stove

❄ A grown-up to help

3. Using a spoon, empty the snow from the measuring cup into the pot. Heat the snow until it melts. Ask a grown-up to pour the water from the pot back into the measuring cup. Did the water level come up to the same line that the snow did? Are you surprised at the amount of water you have? Write down your results.

Try It Again

Try the big thaw experiment after another snowfall. You might find that you have more or less water after you melt your snow than the last time you did the experiment. How can this be? Well, the amount of moisture in snow varies depending on the weather conditions during the snowfall. You might find very little water in a snow that fell when the temperature was above 32 degrees (0° Celsius). Generally, the rule of thumb is that for every 10 inches (25 centimeters) of snow there would be 1 inch (2.5 centimeters) of rain or water. Sometimes that can change to as high as 28 inches (71 centimeters) of snow to only 1 inch (2.5 centimeters) of water or as low as 6 inches (15 centimeters) of snow to only 1 inch (2.5 centimeters) of water.

SNOWFLAKE STUDY

1 or more kids

Snowflakes are first formed with the creation of snow crystals. These snow crystals are created when water vapor becomes deposited on a very tiny particle called an ice nucleus, or when the ice nucleus causes tiny droplets of supercooled water to freeze. This nucleus may be a dust particle from a farmer's field, a particle of exhaust gas from a car, or a tiny splinter of ice broken off of another falling snow crystal. The six-sided crystals then develop and grow in a pattern depending on the temperature of the air and the humidity level. Some look like columns, others like dinner plates.

Snowflakes are created when these ice crystals, both whole and broken, join together while falling through the sky. Sometimes as many as 100 ice crystals cling together to form a snowflake. Each snowflake can be as much as an inch to three inches in diameter, depending on how many ice crystals join together. Flakes are sometimes a simple shape, but often a snowflake is a complex star with beautiful details.

Step outside during a snowfall and you will have a museumful of crystals to study—and no two are alike!

What You Do

1. Step outside with your dark paper or cloth and begin collecting snowflakes.

2. Take a look at the flakes you have collected. What shapes do the snowflakes have in common?

3. Continue collecting flakes on your cloth or paper. If you have a ruler, see if you can find and measure the largest snowflake you have collected. If you have a handheld lens, take a look at the snowflakes under the lens. Try drawing one of the snowflakes that you have studied.

17

PAPER SNOWFLAKES

I or more kids

ow that you have studied real snowflakes outside, try making some out of paper to hang inside your house.

WHAT YOU NEED

Square sheets of paper

Scissors

❄ **A grown-up to help**

What You Do

1. Take a square piece of paper. Fold the paper in half and in half again.

2. Fold the sides of the small square into the middle. Fold one side up to create a triangle.

3. Now comes the fun part. Cut shapes into the folded triangle. Be sure not to cut the entire length of a folded edge.

4. Open up your paper. Do you have a six-sided snowflake or a more creative variation? If your snowflake came apart when you opened it, try again, being careful not to cut the entire length of the folded edge.

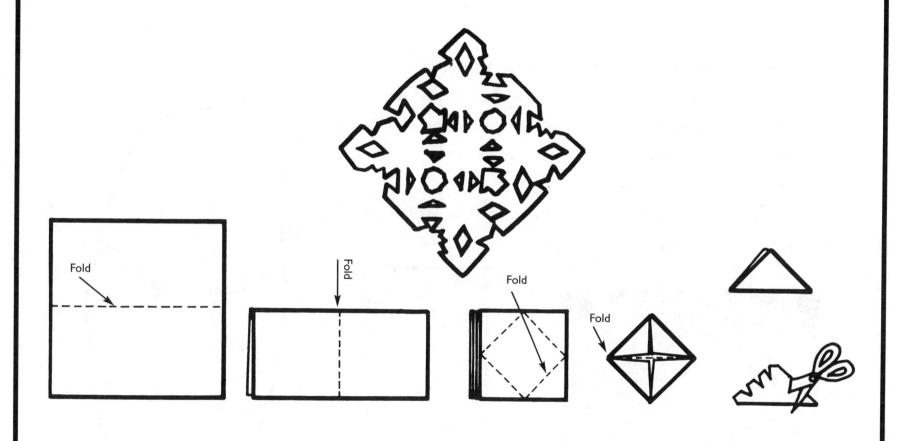

Fold

Fold

Fold

Fold

SNOWSHOES

I or more kids

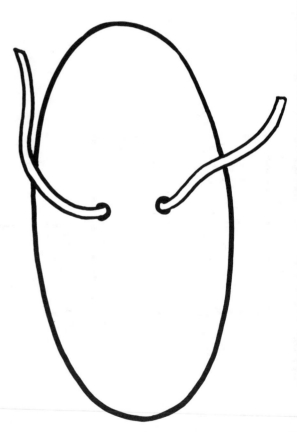

Snowshoes make it easy to walk on soft snow. They spread your weight out over the surface, which keeps you from sinking down into the snow. Strapping on a pair of snowshoes is perfect for a winter walk in the woods or a short race with your friends.

Check out a nearby nature center for snowshoe rentals, or make your own.

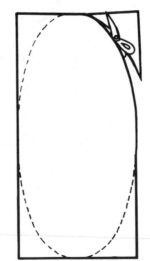

WHAT YOU NEED

Large cardboard box

Pencil

Ruler

Scissors

Twine or elastic

❄ **A grown-up to help**

What You Do

1. Ask a grown-up to help you cut out two large ovals from the cardboard. The ovals should be roughly 12 inches (30 centimeters) wide by 24 inches (60 centimeters) long.

2. Place a foot in the middle of each of the cut ovals. Have the grown-up use the scissors to poke two holes in the center of each of the ovals, on either side of your foot.

3. Thread the elastic or twine up through the bottom of the holes so that the two ends are on the top of the oval.

Snowshoes Step Up

When Native Americans and Eskimos used snow-shoes for transportation hundreds of years ago, they made them out of wood and animal skins. Nowadays you can find snowshoes made not only of wood, but also of aluminum and other light-weight materials, with styles called bear claw, Michigan, Alaskan, and Maine.

4. Place your foot on the oval and tie the twine around your foot. Step up with the oval on your foot. Does the oval stay on? If it does, you are ready to step out into the snow with your very own snowshoes.

MARVELOUS MAPLE SYRUP SENSATIONS

I or more kids

Try making these tasty treats on clean, fresh-fallen snow.

What You Do

1. Pour the maple syrup into the saucepan.

2. Ask a grown-up to help you warm the syrup on a stove. Do not boil the syrup.

3. Take the warm syrup outside to a patch of fresh snow. Pat the snow down a little bit to create a nice, flat surface to make your maple treats.

4. With the wooden spoon, drizzle the warm syrup onto the snow. Watch the syrup harden right before your eyes.

5. Try making different shapes or writing your name in the snow with the syrup. When you're finished, sample your homemade maple candy. Tastes yummy, doesn't it?

Sugaring Time

The sap of the sugar maple trees begins to flow when the winter freeze stops and thawing begins in late winter and early spring. It takes roughly 40 gallons (180 liters) of collected sugar maple sap to produce one gallon of maple syrup. Many farms invite visitors to watch their maple syrup production. Check with your local cooperative extension service for local sugar houses that produce maple syrup.

FUN AND GAMES

Here's some fun for you to try,

So grab a friend and out you fly.

BASKET "SNOW" BALL

I or more kids

If you are missing your basketball hoop this winter, here's a game that you will love.

What You Do

1. Place the clothes basket on a flat surface of snow.

2. Stand a few feet from the basket and make a snowball. Pitch the snowball into the basket. Get your friends together and take some practice shots.

3. When you're ready to start your game, gather your friends and have them each make a snowball. Each player stands three steps away from the basket and takes turns throwing the snowballs into the basket. Did everyone make the basket? All the players who have tossed their snowballs successfully into the basket take three

more steps back from the basket. Take turns shooting baskets again with new snowballs.

4. Each player continues to shoot baskets, moving three steps back from the basket each time they toss a snowball in the basket. The farthest one from the basket after everyone else has missed their shots wins the game.

HOOPS

I or more kids

Do you have an old hula hoop lying around just waiting for the warm weather? Well, dig it out and play a game of hoops. It's a great way to practice your aim for spring Little League.

What You Do

1. Place the hula hoop in the snow so that it can stand up facing you. Form some snowballs to throw through the hoop. Practice throwing farther and farther from the hoop.

2. Tie yarn around a pinecone, leaving about a 12-inch (30 centimeters) tail of yarn.

3. Attach the tail of yarn to the top of the hula hoop so that the pinecone hangs into the middle of the hoop.

4. Make a snowball and see if you can hit the pinecone. Is it easy or hard? If it's easy, you might just have the aim to pitch this spring.

Hula Hoop Craze

Kids have been playing with hoops for centuries, but it took Richard Knerr and Arthur "Spud" Melin, the founders of the Wham-O Company, to propel the hoop into the twentieth century. After hearing about Australian kids who twirled hoops around their waists in gym class, they developed the modern hula hoop. It hit the stores in 1958. Sales reached 25 million in the first two months. This fad is still going strong. Who would have thought the hula hoop was destined to become an American classic?

KNOCK 'EM OVER

1 or more kids

Don't bring that clothes basket inside yet. This game is a carryover from one that you've probably seen at a summer fair. Imagine a Ferris wheel nearby and plenty of cotton candy instead of snow. Summer is not too far away!

What You Do

1. Place the clothes basket upside down to create a flat surface above the snow. You can also use a picnic table or other available surface.

2. Fill the cups with good packing snow and turn them over onto the flat area of the basket. These will be your targets. Place the targets close to each other. You may even want to stack them into a pyramid.

3. Get a bunch of your friends together and see who can knock down the snow targets with a snowball. Can you find the best place to hit the targets to make them all fall at once?

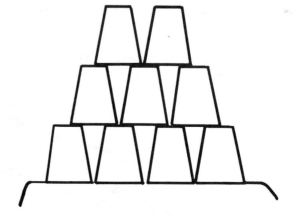

WINTER DAY PICNIC

1 or more kids

Make a Snow Picnic Table

Your picnic table is probably under a lot of snow or packed away until summer. Don't let that stop you. Use the snow to make your own table for your picnic.

What You Do

1. With the help of a grown-up and good packing snow, you are on your way to making your own picnic table. First, ask a grown-up to shovel a circle in the snow but to leave the center for you to use as a table.

2. Carve out areas in the snow around the table to use as seats. Gently pack the snow down.

3. Add a tablecloth by spreading your picnic blanket on the snow table. You are ready for your picnic.

Picnic Treats to Pack

Looking for perfect snowy-day picnic treats? Here are some picnic packing tips for your next winter picnic. Don't forget to pack extras in case friends drop by.

WHAT YOU NEED

Picnic basket

Bowls, cups, napkins, and spoons or forks

Aluminum foil

1 thermos or more

What You Do

1. Plan your picnic menu. Hot foods taste best on a cold winter day. Include a hot soup or chili, hot cocoa, and warm muffins.

2. To keep your food warm until you're ready to eat, make sure everything is wrapped well in aluminum foil or kept hot in a thermos. Try to keep the food inside until your table is ready.

3. Pack your basket and head outside to your picnic spot.

Chase the Chills Chili

Here's a recipe for a chili that is sure to keep you toasty warm on a winter day.

What You Do

1. Ask a grown-up to slice the green peppers, onions, and garlic.

2. Sauté the green peppers and garlic in the butter. When they are nearly brown, add the onions.

3. Continue to sauté the peppers, onion, and garlic until brown, then add the ground beef or chicken.

4. Sauté until the meat is brown, then reduce the heat.

5. Add the cumin, chili powder, beans, and enough red wine vinegar until you can smell it in the pot.

WHAT YOU NEED

¼ cup (60 ml) butter

2 mild green peppers

4 cloves garlic

4 to 6 medium onions

1 ½ to 2 pounds (.7 to .9 kg) lean ground beef or chicken

1 tablespoon (15 ml) cumin

4 tablespoons (60 ml) chili powder

2 cans kidney beans or other beans

Red wine vinegar

2 tablespoons (30 ml) cocoa powder

2 tablespoons (30 ml) honey

Salt and pepper to taste

Stockpot

Optional toppings: sour cream, grated cheese, diced onions or scallions, and/or green peppers

❄ A grown-up to help

Makes 4 to 6 servings

6. Let the mixture simmer for at least 45 minutes. Add the cocoa powder and honey and allow to simmer an additional 10 to 15 minutes.

7. Taste the chili and add salt and pepper if desired. Be sure to pack toppings to add to your chili, and a warm corn muffin for a yummy treat.

SNOWY DAY BINGO

3 or more kids

When it's too cold to play outdoors, grab some friends and play this fun game of bingo.

WHAT YOU NEED

Ruler

Markers

Cardboard or construction paper

Pencil

Scissors

A handful of buttons, beans, or other game markers for each player

Paper cup or other container

What You Do

1. To create the game board, each player needs a ruler, marker, and paper. Use the ruler to measure four columns the length of the paper and four columns across the paper. The completed game board should have 16 squares.

2. In each square, using your pencil, draw or write the words for these snowy day items or others you choose: snowflake, snowman, pine tree, scarf, snow day, mitten, snowshoe, Valentine's Day, Season's Greetings, skis, boots, bird feeder, sled, hot cocoa, snowball, and icicle. Draw or write these words in random order on your game board.

3. The caller copies each word or drawing on a separate piece of paper, cuts them out, and places them in a container.

4. To play the game: The caller draws each word out, one at a time. When the caller announces a word, the players look for that item on their game boards and place a marker on that square. The first player to complete a row, either horizontally, vertically, or diagonally, wins the game.

I Spy Snow

It's a lot of fun to take a winter walk. While you're walking, see what you can spy with your little eye. Take a short break from your walk and look around. Choose someone to go first. Start with "I spy with my little eye . . ." and then name something you see. The first person who sees what you are looking at gets to go next. Walk to another spot and play another round. Pack a thermos of hot cocoa to enjoy while you're playing.

FOOTPRINT TAG

2 or more kids

Footprint tag is a great game to play with a friend after a snowfall. So, before the snow gets stamped on by anyone else, put on your boots, grab a friend, and head outside.

What You Do

1. Pick a wide area of clean, untrampled snow. Count to 10. While you are counting, the other players must walk or run through the clean snow, leaving only footprints behind. No fair running backward!

2. This is not an ordinary game of tag, because the trick is to not only catch the other people but to stay in their footprints while you chase them. Make sure you start on the same foot that they did. Can you tell when they walked and when they ran by the size of their footprints? Which ones are harder to follow?

3. The persons being chased can wind around and walk in figure eights, making it very difficult for the chaser to follow their footprints.

4. Switch roles and play again.

More Fun with Footprints

Check out Snowprints and Signs on page 48 for some activities you can do with animal footprints.

MITTEN MADNESS

3 or more kids

This game proves that mittens don't have to just keep your hands warm in the cold. Here is a fun game that you can play with your mittens and some friends when you're out of the cold.

What You Do

1. Roll each mitten up into a ball. Fold the cuff over the ball to keep it rolled.

2. Fold the bedsheet in half. Place the mittens in the middle of the sheet.

3. Pick up the sheet and have everyone hold onto a corner.

4. While holding onto the sheet, move your arms back and forth and up and down, so that the sheet is set in motion. The object is to knock off all the mittens but your own. The game continues until only one mitten remains. The player whose mitten remains is the winner.

SNOW SNAKE GAME

2 or more kids

This game is a variation of a Native American game that is played during the winter. It is usually played on ice, but it can be played in soft snow, as it is here.

What You Do

1. Each player takes three to five smooth sticks. With a marker or paint, decorate one end of the stick with the features of a snake. The sticks are then marked at the other end with paint or markers, the first with one line, the second with two lines, the third with three, and so on.

2. Ask a grown-up to shovel a space in your yard or alley that is at least 12 feet (3.6 meters) long.

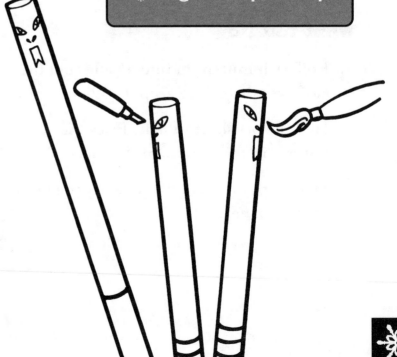

38

3. All the players stand in a line at one end of the cleared space. Each player throws a stick headfirst down the alley. The player whose stick goes the farthest adds up the marks on all the other sticks to obtain his score. Those sticks are then put aside and each player throws a new stick down the alley.

4. After all the sticks have been thrown, the player with the highest score wins the game. Does this game remind you of bowling? Bowling is another great way to spend a winter day.

LAYER UP RELAY

4 or more kids

H it the closet and take out your winter clothes for this great relay game. When you finish playing, you will be all set to head outdoors for more fun in the snow.

What You Do

1. Pick two or more teams for the relay, line up, and place a pile of clothes at the end of each team's row. The pile should include all of the players' outdoor clothing, including boots, coats, hats, and mittens.

2. On the count of three, the first person on each team runs over to the pile of clothes and looks for an article of his own clothing. The player puts it on, runs back to his team, and tags the next person.

3. The next player runs to the pile and finds the same article of clothing among her clothes. She puts it on, runs back, and tags the next person. For example, if the first player ran to the pile, found his coat, and put it on, then the second player must find her coat, put it on, and so on.

4. The game continues until all players are wearing all their outdoor clothing. The first team to complete dressing wins. Now you are all ready to head outside into the snow!

CUTTING THE PIE

3 or more kids

This game is a favorite in the Midwest. Some may know it by the name Fox and Geese, but since the playing field looks like a giant pie, we prefer Cutting the Pie. After you are finished playing, invite everyone in for a slice of your favorite pizza or fruit pie.

What You Do

1. Form a line with your friends and stomp out a big circle in the snow to form the pie crust.

2. Stand around the circle and mark it off into pie sections by walking across the circle. The more sections, the better off the Pie Man will be.

3. All of the players gather around the circle. One person is chosen to be the Pie Man.

4. The Pie Man is only allowed to run on all the stomped-down lines from the center to the crust to catch the players, but the players can only run on the outer stomped circle or the pie crust. If the Pie Man tags a player, that player becomes the next Pie Man and the game begins again.

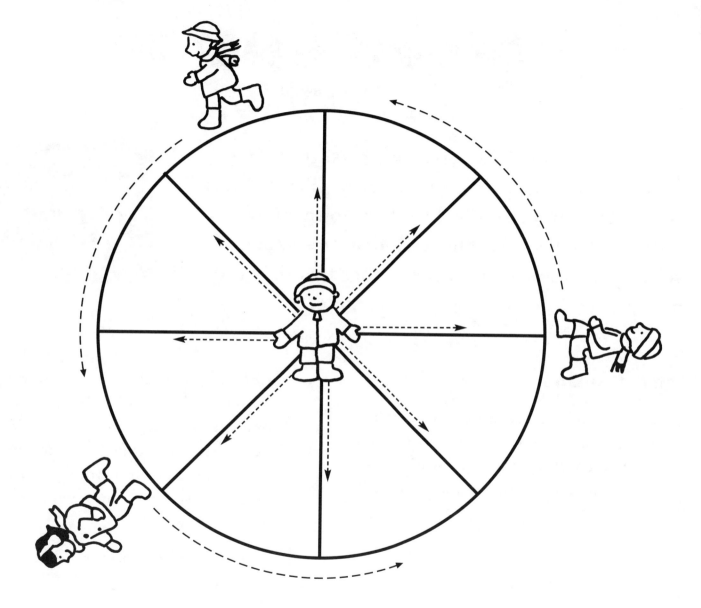

GOING ONE UP

4 or more kids

Kids in colonial America enjoyed throwing snowballs, skating, and sledding just as much as you do. They also liked to slide down snowy hills, so much so that they made up this game. When you are playing it, remember that they did not have snowpants to help them slide.

WHAT YOU NEED

A bunch of your friends

A snowy hill

What You Do

1. Line up behind each other at the top of the hill. One by one, sit down and slide down the hillside. After a few people slide down the hill, a nice, smooth track will form.

2. Line up again. One by one, everyone should sit down and slide down the hill one after the other. The object of the game is to try to touch the heels of your feet to the slider in front of you. If you do touch, you get to move ahead of that person in the line.

3. Continue to see who can become the next line leader.

Colonial Holiday

The New York Colony celebrated First Skating Day each winter. Businesses were closed so everyone could enjoy a day of ice skating. Don't you wish that we still celebrated that holiday?

WINTER CRITTERS

Tiny footprints you will find

In the snow, the critter kind.

SNOWPRINTS AND SIGNS

I or more kids

Every morning after a snowfall you will find evidence of the critters that inhabit the winter world around us. You may find a path across your lawn, or maybe tiny little marks on a snow-covered windowsill. If you are careful, you can play detective and find out what animals are busy looking for food when you are sleeping.

WHAT YOU NEED box

WHAT YOU NEED

Tape measure

What You Do

1. If you live in the country or a suburb, take a look outside your window the morning after a snowfall. (Visit a local park if you live in a city.) What do you see? You might see crisscrossing trails of footprints winding around in the snow. You might see clumps of disturbed snow underneath a tree. Look carefully. What signs of animal life can you find?

2. Animal footprints or tracks come in many different sizes, just like their owners. You might see tiny bird tracks or large deer tracks. Sometimes the size of the track is different from the size of the hoof or foot of the animal that created it. Take a look at your own footprints in the snow. Use a tape measure to measure your track, then measure your boot. Are they the same?

3. Use the guide below to identify the animal tracks you find. How many different tracks can you identify?

4. Try making different types of tracks in the snow. Pretend you are a rabbit hopping through the snow. What do your tracks look like? Take a look in a field guide and see if rabbit tracks are similar. Pretend you are a fox, walking in a very straight line, like a tightrope. What do your tracks look like?

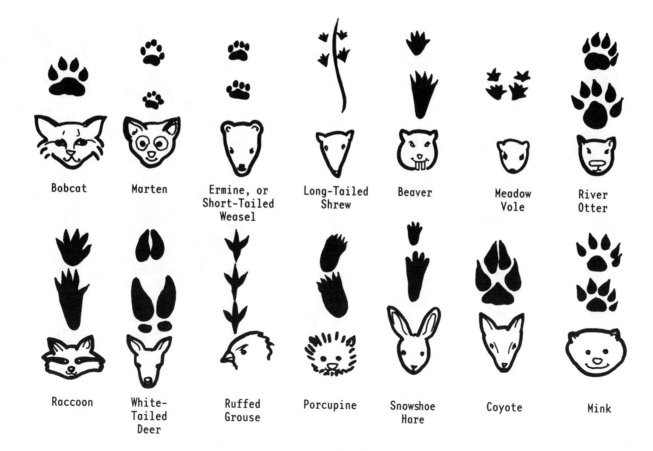

Bobcat Marten Ermine, or Short-Tailed Weasel Long-Tailed Shrew Beaver Meadow Vole River Otter

Raccoon White-Tailed Deer Ruffed Grouse Porcupine Snowshoe Hare Coyote Mink

WINTER NIGHTS

1 or more kids

If you have never enjoyed a winter night, then this is the time to start. Yes, it is cold out there, but the wonders that you can see clearly make up for it. So, bundle up and head outside. Don't forget to bring a grown-up!

Starry, Starry Night

What can you expect to see in the winter sky besides the moon? Stars, of course! But what else?

What You Do

1. Before the sun sets completely, go to an area that does not have a lot of lights from buildings or cars. Set up your folding chairs or spread out your blanket in an area that gives you a clear view of the sky.

2. Look just above the western horizon shortly after sunset and you will find the planet Venus. Planets look like stars in the night sky. Venus is the closest planet to Earth and is often called the Evening Star. It will look like a bright star. Did you find it?

3. As it begins to get darker, take a look all around the night sky. As you already found out, not all those shimmering points of light you see in the sky are stars. If you are lucky, you might see what looks like a shooting star. Shooting stars are really meteors that fall through Earth's atmosphere. Sometimes they fly through the night sky so fast that you may think that you didn't even see them. If you do see one, be sure to make a wish. It just might come true.

4. Although there are twinkling lights in the sky that are not stars, the majority of the lights you see are stars. It is fun to look up at the stars and look for the pictures they form, which are called *constellations*. You can look for the Big Dipper, which is part of the constellation Great Bear, or the Little Dipper, which resembles the Big Dipper but contains the North Star at the end of its handle.

Moon Walk

When the moon is full and snow covers the ground, grab a grown-up and take a walk outside. You will be amazed at what you see and hear. So move over, Michael Jackson and John Glenn, this is a different kind of moon walk.

What You Do

1. Dress warmly and wear sturdy shoes or boots for your moon walk. Check the batteries in your flashlight and head out before it gets dark so that you will be familiar with your surroundings. Look for an area that does not have a lot of light from signs or buildings. The darker the area, the easier it will be for you to see the winter sky.

2. Stand still or sit down on a stump for a short while. Listen to the sounds of the evening. Do you hear sounds that you do not hear during the day? Which ones can you identify? How does the air smell? How far can you see by the light of the full moon?

Whooooo Goes There?

January is the perfect time to go owling. You may not always see or hear an owl, but it is still a wonderful way to spend a moonlit winter evening.

What You Do

1. Before you start out for the evening, look around the area during the day. Look for wooded areas that border fields. If you find whitewash on trees or owl pellets underneath, it is a sure sign that owls are around.

2. Head to the same spot in the evening. Arrive there just before dark. Use an owl hooter or make your own owl calls to attract them, then sit back and wait. At home, enjoy reading Jane Yolen's *Owl Moon* for a great owling tale.

Owl Pellets

Owl pellets are the equivalent of a cat's hairball. This small, oval-shaped pellet contains the bits of bone and fur that the owl is unable to digest. The owl spits up the pellet just as a cat spits up a hairball. By taking the pellet apart, we are able to identify what the owl has eaten. There might be tiny bones from a mouse or the skull of a mole compacted with bits of the animal's fur in the pellet.

BIRD BUFFET TREE

1 or more kids

Many birds find it difficult to find food during the cold winter months. Many rely on bird feeders and berries that still remain on bare tree branches. Serve up a grand buffet for your feathered friends this winter that they are sure to love, while also giving them added shelter against the cold.

What You Do

1. Prop up your old Christmas tree in your yard after the holidays, or pick out a tree to decorate in your yard that has sturdy branches and areas for the birds to find shelter.

2. Ask a grown-up to thread a needle and knot the thread for you, if you need help. String the popcorn in long strands of garland. You can also add pieces of bread, donuts, or cranberries between the popcorn. Set the garlands aside.

WHAT YOU NEED

Used Christmas tree (optional)

Needle and thread

Popcorn

Bread

Donuts

Cranberries

Peanut butter

Pinecones

Birdseed

Orange

Yarn

❄ A grown-up to help

54

3. Spread the peanut butter on the pinecone with your fingers. Roll the pinecone in the bird seed. Attach a string or yarn around the top to hang it. Set it aside.

4. Cut the orange in half. Ask a grown-up to scoop the orange out of the skin of each half, leaving two empty orange bowls. Have the grown-up make a hole on each side of the orange bowl. Thread yarn through the holes for a hanger.

5. Spread peanut butter on the inside of the bowl and fill with birdseed. Set aside.

6. Assemble any other items you would like to use to decorate your bird buffet. Perhaps you have donuts to hang, or suet treats. Carry them all outside and begin decorating the tree with all the bird treats. Space them evenly around the tree so that the birds can enjoy them from all directions. Head back inside and watch your tree. It will take the birds a little while to notice your treats, so keep a

Wassail

On January 6, people in the British countryside think about nature. Farmers used to gather around the largest, oldest tree that had given them fruit over the years. They sang songs and did a stamping dance to remind the tree to reawaken in spring, and they drank hot, spiced cider called "wassail." It is similar to the spiced cider that is enjoyed during the Chinese New Year. Look on page 124 for the recipe.

lookout. Once they find them, they will be filling nearby shrubs and trees waiting for their chance at the natural feeders you have made for them.

7. Keep a record of the birds that visit your tree. How many different types of birds visit your bird buffet? How many days are they able to enjoy your treats before you need to hang some new ones? Use a field guide to keep track of the different birds you see. Which birds seem a bit timid? Which birds seem bold? Which birds return often? Which eat in groups?

BEAR PAJAMA PARTY

2 or more kids

Y ou might agree with the bears that winter is a great time to stay cozy at home and hibernate until spring; but you may find it a bit hard, especially if you need to go to school. Instead of sleeping all winter, try a bear pajama party with your family or friends.

WHAT YOU NEED

Berry Bear Punch
Beary Muffins

The Details

Hold your party in an area where you can spread out your sleeping bags and play games. When everyone arrives, get right into your pj's, pull out your favorite stuffed bear, and get ready for fun. There are so many things you can do during your bear pajama party. Take turns reading your favorite bear stories or watch a bear video (see page 61 for some suggestions) while you munch on muffins drizzled with honey. Remember to give everyone a bear hug good-night!

The Music

Choose some *beary* nice music to play at your party, like "The Bear Went Over the Mountain" or songs from Winnie-the-Pooh for starters. You might want to hand out the words and have your own sing-along.

Berry Bear Punch

What You Do

1. Pour the can of ginger ale into the ice cube tray. Place a raspberry in each cube. Place in the freezer and allow a few hours to freeze.

2. Pour the bottles of juice into the punch bowl. Add the ginger ale.

3. Remove the ice cubes from the tray and add them to the punch bowl.

4. Ladle the punch into the cups and enjoy your berry delicious drink!

WHAT YOU NEED

Ginger ale, 1 bottle or 1 can

Ice cube tray

1 pint (550 ml) raspberries

2 32-ounce (.9 kg) bottles fruit juice (cherry, cranberry, or other berry flavor)

Punch bowl

Ladle

Cups

❄ A grown-up to help

Makes 8 servings

Beary Muffins

What You Do

1. In one mixing bowl, cream butter and 1 ¼ cup sugar together.

2. Add honey and stir.

3. Add eggs, one at a time, and beat well.

4. Sift dry ingredients (flour, salt, and baking powder) into the second bowl. Slowly add the dry mixture to the other (wet) mixture, alternating with milk.

5. Fold the berries into the batter.

6. Place the cupcake liners in the muffin pan and spoon batter into each cup. Sprinkle with remaining sugar.

7. Ask a grown-up to turn on the oven for you. Bake at 375° F (190° C) until golden brown, approximately 25 minutes. Serve warm with a smidgen of honey.

Great Bear Books and Videos

Books

Bond, Michael. *A Bear Called Paddington*. New
York: Houghton Mifflin Co., 1998.

Carlstrom, Nancy White. *How Do You Say It
Today, Jesse Bear?* New York: Simon &
Schuster, 1992.

Martin, Bill. *Brown Bear, Brown Bear, What Do You
See?* New York: Henry Holt & Co., 1992.

Milne, A. A. *The Best of Winnie-the-Pooh*. New
York: Penguin, 1997.

Videos

*Winnie-the-Pooh and the Blustery Day, The Adventures
of Paddington Bear,* and *Bear in the Big Blue House*
are bound to be favorites at your party.

For a realistic look at a bear's life, watch *The
Bear.*

Don't Wake the Bear

Bears do not sleep soundly all through the winter. When they are hibernating, their bodies slow down, which enables them to save energy. Unlike some other animals, like groundhogs, bears occasionally get up while they are hibernating and may even leave their dens. Winter is also the time when cubs are born in the den.

This old favorite is a great game to play during your pajama party. Just remember when you are playing that bears do not sleep soundly.

WHAT YOU NEED

Open playing area to run

3 or more kids

What You Do

1. Choose one person to be the bear. The bear should crouch in the middle of your playing area with eyes closed, just like a hibernating bear.

2. Slowly and carefully, the players creep from one side of the playing area to the other side, being careful not to wake the sleeping bear.

3. If the bear wakes up while you are crossing, the players quickly run from the bear to the other side of the playing area without getting tagged by the bear. If the bear tags a player, that player becomes a bear too.

4. The tagged bears hibernate in the center of the playing area and the play continues. Only the last tagged bear wakes up to chase the players. The other bears remain hibernating. Players need to remember who was the last player tagged.

5. The winner of the game is the only person left untagged.

The Teddy Bear

Ask your parents if they had a favorite teddy bear when they were small. Chances are they did. People have been collecting and loving teddy bears for a while. Teddy bears first became popular in the early 1900s when President Theodore Roosevelt refused to shoot a bear during a hunting trip. The story became widely known and soon a man named Morris Michtom in New York asked President Roosevelt if he could use his name for the stuffed bears he made. It's a good thing the president said yes, because teddy bears have been popular ever since. Do you think they would be as popular if we called them Morris bears?

SNOWSHOE HARE PUPPET

I or more kids

The snowshoe hare lives in the northern part of the United States and throughout Canada. Unlike the common cottontail rabbit, the snowshoe hare has the ability to change color. In the warm months it is brown and in the winter it becomes white. This is very helpful to the hare when it's trying to escape from other animals. It's able to *camouflage* itself. That means that it blends in with the snow-covered ground and is difficult to find.

There are many other interesting things about the snowshoe hare. For example, it can run up to 27 MPH (43 KPH) and can jump 10 feet (3 meters) in a single hop!

WHAT YOU NEED

I sheet stiff white felt

Scissors

Craft glue

I mitten

I pair googly eyes

White pipe cleaners

I white pom-pom or cotton ball

❄ A grown-up to help

Snowshoes

The snowshoe hare doesn't really wear snowshoes, of course, but it does have feet that enable it to hop and run well in the snow, just like snowshoes. Strapping on a real pair of snowshoes is a fun way to take a winter walk in the snow. If you don't own any snowshoes, call a local wildlife center or outdoor store. They might have snowshoes that you can borrow or rent. Or try making your own. Look on page 20 for directions.

The next time you lose a mitten, make this great snowshoe hare puppet with the mitten that didn't get lost.

What You Do

1. Ask a grown-up to help you cut out two bunny ears from the white felt. Glue them to the top side of the mitten (that covers the back of the hand) halfway down the hand.

2. Glue the googly eyes on the top side near the fingertips.

3. Poke the pipe cleaners through the fingertips end of the mitten right underneath the eyes to create the whiskers of the hare.

4. Glue the pom-pom to the side near the thumb to create the tail.

5. Cut a small triangle out of the felt and glue it over the front of the whiskers to create a nose.

Your snowshoe hare puppet is finished. See if you can make up a story to act out with your puppet. What other animals could you make out of your old mittens?

DEER DETECTIVE

1 or more kids

Deer wintering areas are called "deeryards." You might have a perfect deeryard for local deer close to where you live. Do you know of a nearby grove of thick evergreens that are over 30 feet (9.1 meters) tall? If your answer is yes, you might indeed have an ideal wintering area for deer. The evergreens provide a barrier against the cold winter winds. They also tend to catch a lot of the snow, so that the area does not get as much snow on the ground, which helps the deer find food.

Deeryards are not the only places for deer in the winter. How can we tell if a deer is nearby? See if you can spot the clues and be a deer detective.

WHAT YOU NEED

A wooded area

What You Do

1. Keep a watch out for deer tracks.

2. Since deer do not have upper teeth, only bottom, they must scrape and tear at branches for food. Look for low branches that they have scraped and broken for food.

3. Look for deer droppings, called *scat*. They resemble piles of small, brown pellets.

4. Look for scrapings on trees where a male deer might have rubbed his antlers.

5. Look for bits of deer fur that might have caught on low bushes.

6. What can you conclude from your findings? Do you think there are deer around? Did you find any other clues?

Way up north in the land
of ice and snow

Are adventures and fun
to get to know.

67

ICE FLOE

4 or more kids

This Canadian game is named after the floating sheets of sea ice that are found in the far north. Some of the sheets of ice can be five or more miles across. Others can be quite small. Here's a chance to pretend you are floating through the Arctic Ocean on an ice floe with your friends.

WHAT YOU NEED

Newspaper
Large, open playing area

What You Do

1. The object of the game is for one team to advance across the playing area on the ice floe before the other team. To start, divide the players into two equal-sized teams.

2. Each team takes two sheets of newspaper. The newspaper is the team's ice floe.

3. Each team places one sheet of newspaper down in front of it and then everyone from that team stands on the ice floe.

4. The second sheet of newspaper should be given to the team. Each team places the second sheet of newspaper in front of it.

5. When the second sheet is on the floor, the whole team must move to that sheet. When they have all stepped onto the second ice floe, they should reach behind them and pick up the first newspaper.

6. Each team continues across the playing field by placing a sheet in front and then picking up the one behind. Newspapers tear easily, which adds more excitement to the game, as the players try to move carefully while still keeping up their speed.

7. The team that reaches the other side first while staying on its ice floe wins the game.

Home on an Ice Floe

Would you like to make your home on an ice floe? If you were a polar bear or a walrus, you would. It may not seem like a paradise, but for a polar bear there are seals to eat and for walruses, a banquet of sea snails, shrimp, fish, and sea urchins. Since walruses and polar bears often inhabit the same ice floe, conflicts often occur. The walruses usually have the advantage in the water, but the bears do a bit better on the ice.

NORTHERN LIGHTS SCRATCHBOARD

I or more kids

The northern lights, or *aurora borealis*, look like waves of color in the night sky. The farther north you travel, the greater your chance of catching a glimpse of them. Here's a way for you to create their beauty right at home so that you don't have to travel to the Arctic.

WHAT YOU NEED

Poster board or other heavy paper stock

Oil pastels

Paper clip

What You Do

1. Color the entire surface of the paper with a variety of oil pastels, making sure you use green, blue, yellow, and red.

2. Take a black pastel and color over the entire colored paper.

3. Use the paper clip to scratch through the black pastel and release the colors underneath. Photographs of the northern lights often reveal ripples, curls, and what look like curtains of light. Your picture can have any or all of these.

For Older Kids

Make up your own tale to explain the dancing northern lights, then find out what really causes these lights to appear around the North and South Poles.

SOAPSTONE SCULPTURES

1 or more kids

The native Inuit people of the Arctic have long relied on their skill in carving bone and stone to create the tools, bowls, and other items needed for everyday life. Their carving skill can also be seen in the beautiful sculptures that they create using easy-to-carve soapstone. Soapstone is a rock that is found worldwide and varies in color. It has a soapy feel to it, hence the name "soapstone."

WHAT YOU NEED

3 cups Ivory Snow detergent

¾ cup (180 ml) water

Bowl

Electric mixer

The Inuit artists have been using soapstone to capture everyday life in the Arctic for many years. Their sculptures reflect the nature and people that surround them, such as seals, polar bears, whales, hunters, and Inuit mothers. The smooth, soft stone becomes their canvas as they carve simple designs that leave room for imagination. Here's a way to create your own sculpture using real soap instead of soapstone.

What You Do

1. Place the Ivory Snow and the water in a bowl.

2. Use the electric mixer to combine until the soap becomes doughy.

3. Remove the mixture from the bowl. Now you are ready to mold your faux soapstone. Pick an Inuit subject, or something that reflects your everyday life. Scoop out a handful of the soap clay.

4. Try to create your figure using one piece of soap clay without adding any pieces to your figure. Model the soap by pushing and pulling the figure into shape. Keep in mind the simple shapes of Inuit sculptures.

5. Allow your sculpture to air dry overnight. Once it is dry, it will be a bright white and hard to the touch. Use your imagination to create other shapes.

More on Soapstone

Soapstone varies in color. It can be variations of green, brown, or gray. Egyptians, Asians, and Africans, as well as Inuits, use this stone for carving. They use a variety of carving and sanding tools to achieve their designs. Do you think all soapstone artists carve the same subjects? Would an artist in Africa carve a polar bear? Explore soapstone sculptures created by different native people and see if you can find any differences or similarities. A number of Web sites on soapstone can be found in "Favorite Winter Books, Videos, and Web Sites" on page 145.

INUIT CLAY BIRD GAME

3 or more kids

Inuit children in the frozen north play this game with small birds that they have carved out of bone. You and your friends will find that making the game is as much fun as playing it!

What You Do

1. Sculpt 15 birds, each roughly an inch long, out of the air-drying clay. Start with a small ball of clay, and pinch out the wings from the sides. Next, pull a little bit of clay from the body to form a head. Pinch a tiny bit of clay, roll it between your fingers, and stick it on the front of the head to form the bird's beak. The finished bird should look like a duck with a flat bottom. Let the birds dry completely. This will take a couple of hours.

2. When the birds are dry, spread the cloth out on the floor to make your playing surface and invite your friends to sit around it.

3. To play the game, the first player picks up all of the birds, shakes them gently, and tosses them onto the cloth. The birds will land in all directions, some upright, some upside down, and some on their sides. If a bird lands upright, the player facing the beak of the bird picks up the bird.

4. The next player picks up all the remaining birds, shakes them, and spills them out on the cloth. All the upright birds are then taken by the players they face. The game continues until all the birds are claimed.

5. The winner is the player who collects the most birds.

REINDEER GAMES

1 or more kids

Imagine a land where the summer sun shines all day and all night. This is the land above the Arctic Circle, sometimes called "The Land of the Midnight Sun." The native people who live there are the Saami. They live in the most northern regions of Norway, Finland, Sweden, Iceland, and Russia. They speak their own language and even have their own flag, even though they live in different countries.

Many Saami herd reindeer. They use the reindeer for many things, just as we use cows. Reindeer are relatives of white-tailed deer. Reindeer become the most talked-about deer during the winter months. You might even see a reindeer in a petting zoo or a Christmas festival this winter. Unlike the white-tailed deer, both male and female reindeer have antlers.

Here's an easy way to draw a reindeer using your very own hands.

WHAT YOU NEED

Newspaper

1 large sheet light-colored construction paper

Brown acrylic or finger paint

Paper plate

Markers

What You Do

1. Cover your craft area with newspaper and place the sheet of construction paper on top.

2. Pour some of the brown paint onto the paper plate. Carefully press each hand into the brown paint.

3. Place your paint-covered hands gently on the paper with your two thumbs almost touching, forming a *V* in the middle. Your prints will create your deer's antlers.

4. Sketch in the deer's head with the markers. Use a *U* shape. Color the tip of the nose black, or if you want to create a Rudolph the Red-Nosed Reindeer picture, color it red.

ESKIMO YO-YO

I or more kids

These yo-yos might be a little different than ones you are accustomed to, but they are packed with fun. In Alaska, yo-yos are generally made of sealskin or polar bear fur and are tied together with a long piece of leather. Some of them are decorated with beautiful beadwork. Here's a way to make an Eskimo yo-yo from things that you probably have in your house. You'll find that making this yo-yo is pretty simple, but playing with it takes practice.

What You Do

1. Ask a grown-up to sew one end of the shoelace firmly to the hacky sack using the tapestry needle. Sew the other end to the second hacky sack.

2. Now you are ready to play with your yo-yo. Hold the cord at a point that is just off center. Let the two balls hang below your hand. Here comes the tricky part: By turning your wrist, see if you can get the two balls to move in opposite directions for as long as possible.

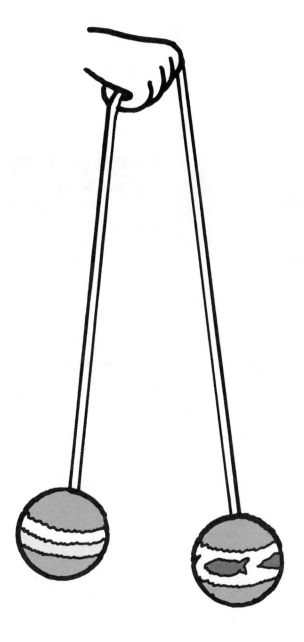

From Weapon to Toy

The yo-yo has a long history with many different cultures. In the 1500s, the yo-yo was used as a weapon in the Philippines. It was not the usual plastic toy we see today, but a stone attached to a long rope. It was used while hunting. The modern yo-yo was brought to the United States in the 1920s by a Filipino named Pedro Flores. He played with his yo-yo during his lunch break as a bellhop in California. A lot of people would stop by to watch him play with his toy, which he named yo-yo, which means "come-come" in Filipino. He soon began to manufacture them. In 1929, Donald Duncan, the founder of Good Humor Ice Cream, bought the company from Pedro Flores. The Duncan Yo-Yo is still the most popular yo-yo on the market. To date, more than 600 million yo-yos have been sold.

SNOW BY ANY OTHER NAME IS STILL SNOW

I or more kids

The Inuit people have over a dozen different words for snow. For example, they call falling snow *anniu* and ground snow *api*. Let's see how many different types of snow you can find outside.

What You Do

1. Can you think of words to describe different kinds of snow? Here are some suggestions: falling snow, crusty snow, and drifting snow. Name some others. Keep these in your mind as you begin.

2. Dress warmly and head outdoors to begin your snowy investigation.

3. Look at the snow around you. Think of words to describe what it looks like.

4. Touch different spots of snow. It will help if you use a bare hand. Does the snow feel smooth, icy, or some other way? How many different kinds of snow can you find?

5. How many different types of snow did you discover on your investigation? Try your investigation on another day and see if you can come up with even more kinds of snow.

MAKE SNOW CREAM

I or more kids

This yummy treat has been made for centuries and is still every bit as delicious when you make it today.

What You Do

1. Use the large bowl and mixing spoon to scoop up some clean snow.

2. Pour the vanilla extract and sugar into the snow.

3. Add the milk and stir the mixture carefully. You might need a little more milk, depending on the size of your bowl.

4. Use the mixing spoon to dish up your yummy snow cream for everyone to taste. Hand out the spoons and dig in!

WHAT YOU NEED

Clean, fresh snow

Large bowl

Mixing spoon

I tablespoon (15 ml) vanilla extract

I cup (230 ml) sugar

⅓ cup (80 ml) milk

Extra bowls and spoons

SPIRIT MASK

I or more kids

Many native people of the Arctic feel especially close to the natural world around them. They rely on the native plants and animals for their survival instead of supermarkets. It is a tradition for hunters to sometimes wear a mask or headdress that resembles an animal before they venture out on a hunt. It is similar to carrying a lucky rabbit's foot. These masks are called "spirit masks." Many native artists now create spirit masks that are meant not to be worn, but to hang on a wall as decoration.

Here's a way to make your own spirit mask of your favorite animal.

WHAT YOU NEED

Paper plate

Markers

Scissors

Craft glue

Feathers, yarn, felt, or other decorations

Stapler

Yarn

✼ A grown-up to help

What You Do

1. Think about your favorite animal. Why do you like this animal? What is it about this animal's spirit that you admire? Is this animal particularly strong? Is it resourceful? Is it loyal, proud, or wise?

2. Find a picture of your animal. Look carefully at the face of your animal. What color are your animal's eyes? Does it have lashes or eyebrows? Does it have whiskers or lips?

3. Turn your paper plate upside down and, using your markers, draw the eyes of your animal in the center of your plate.

4. Ask a grown-up to help you use the scissors to cut out the eyes on your mask so that you will be able to see when you wear it.

5. Decorate the face of your animal with markers. Glue on feathers or felt pieces to add another dimension to your mask. Remember what your animal looks like. Take another look at the picture. What does your animal have that you don't? Does it have a furry face or is it scaly? Think about how you can make your mask look like your favorite animal.

6. When you have finished creating your spirit mask, have a grown-up staple yarn on either side of the mask so that you can tie it on your head.

PAPER PENGUIN

I or more kids

Let's take a trip from the Arctic very far south to Antarctica. What do you think we would find? Are there people living there on the ice and snow as they do in the Arctic way up north? You would be surprised to find that, aside from a few visiting scientists, Antarctica's main residents are the penguins.

Make this quick and easy paper penguin from only five shapes.

WHAT YOU NEED

Black, white, and orange paper

Scissors

Craft glue

Markers

What You Do

1. Using the scissors, cut the white paper into an oval.

2. Create two ovals from the black paper that are the same size as the white one.

3. Cut out a smaller black oval for the head of your penguin and an orange triangle for the beak.

4. Glue the white oval down on a clean sheet of paper. Glue a black oval on either side, overlapping the white oval. Glue the small oval head onto your penguin, followed by the beak.

5. Draw legs and eyes to complete your penguin. What else can you draw around your penguin? Is your penguin standing near the water? Is the sun shining? Think about what it would look like in Antarctica.

IDITAROD RACE RELAY

4 or more kids

It is said in Alaska that men are men and women win the Iditarod. Many of the winners of the Iditarod have been women. The Iditarod is a dogsled race that originated in 1967 to commemorate the dogsled mushers who delivered serum to Nome during a diptheria epidemic in 1927. Without the serum, many people would have died that year. Balto was the famous dog who led the team the 674 miles (1,084 kilometers) from the last train station to Nome, Alaska. Have you heard of him?

The Iditarod takes place every year in Alaska, beginning on the first Saturday in March. Here's a great way to experience the Iditarod race without going to Alaska.

WHAT YOU NEED

Flat snowy surface

Cones or other markers for the racecourse

At least 2 sleds with rope pulls

❄ A grown-up to help

What You Do

1. With the help of a grown-up, create a race-course through a flat snowy area. Place markers at different positions throughout the course.

2. Divide players into two teams, each with an even number of players.

3. Position two players from each team at each of the markers. Two players from each team stay at the starting line. There should be one marker unmanned that will serve as the finish line.

4. Each pair of players decides who is riding in the sled and who pulls the sled.

5. Ask a grown-up to start the race. On the count of three, the first pair from each team begins racing to the first marker.

6. When the team reaches the marker, the team is relieved by the waiting teammates. The next pair of teammates then races to the next marker, and so on.

7. The first team to complete the racecourse is the winning team.

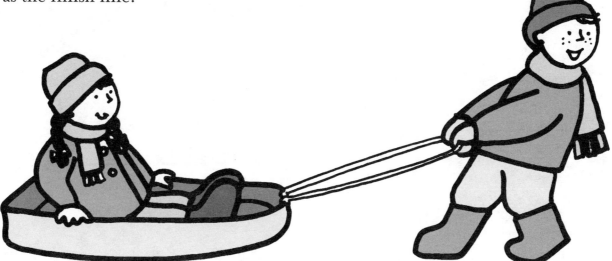

CABIN FEVER

Cocoa, bubbles, and snowflake art

Hurry now and let us start.

SNOW GLOBES

I or more kids

Whether you call them snow globes, snow domes, or shakies, these little worlds in glass or plastic are great fun to collect and make. You have probably seen little snow globes at museums, toy stores, or amusement parks, but did you know that they have been around since the 1800s? They first started out as paperweights in France. Now they are one of the most popular souvenirs.

With a shake of a hand, here's how you can create your own winter wonderland snow globe to be your souvenir of these fun snowy days together.

WHAT YOU NEED

Baby food jar, cleaned, with label removed

Waterproof adhesive (marine glue or similar product)

Small plastic animals and trees

Glitter

Water

½ teaspoon (2.5 ml) vegetable oil or glycerin

Craft glue

❄ A grown-up to help

What You Do

1. With the help of a grown-up, use the waterproof adhesive to attach the animals or trees to the inside lid of the baby food jar, to create your snow globe scene.

2. Add some glitter to the jar and fill it about 2/3 full with water.

3. Add vegetable oil or glycerin to the water.

4. Ask a grown-up to place a little white craft glue on the outside rim of the jar lid, making sure no glue touches the inside of the jar.

5. Screw on the lid of the jar carefully to make sure the glue does not enter the jar. Place the jar in a safe place until the glue dries completely, usually about one hour.

6. After the glue is completely dry, turn your snow globe over and watch it sparkle!

Let's Get Shakin'

Snow globes are one of the easiest souvenirs to collect. Some kids collect snow globes on vacation. They're a great way to remember the cities you visit. Other collectors like the ones that advertise places and products. You can even find your favorite cartoon characters living in the world of snow globes. Snow globe collections can be created out of just about any subject you can dream up.

Need inspiration for your collection? Check out Nancy McMichael's book *Snowdomes* or *Snow Globes* by Connie Moore and Harry Rinker for more information on the history and collecting of these tiny treasures.

Now that you know how to make your own snow globe, you might even want to collect objects from your travels to make your own one-of-a-kind set of souvenir snow globes.

BEANBAG SNOWMAN

I or more kids

When there is not enough snow outside to build a snowman, build one inside. These little snowmen will add a touch of winter to the inside of your whole house this season. Not only will they keep you company, but you can even line them up on a windowsill to keep out cold drafts or use them for a doorstop.

What You Do

1. Turn the sock inside out and fill with beans up to the bottom of the sock band.

2. Wrap the rubber band tightly around the sock to close off the area filled by the beans.

3. Turn down the top of the sock twice to create a cap on the snowman.

4. Tie a ribbon or strip of fabric around the middle of the sock to create the head and middle of the snowman.

5. Now it is time to give your snowman or snowwoman some personality. Add the wiggle eyes with craft glue. You can add any other decorations you like. Tiny buttons or sequins could be added down the front. You can color the cheeks with red marker or draw a mouth. Be creative! You can even make a whole snowman family with different-sized socks.

BEANS

MY MITTEN BOOK

1 or more kids

The next time you come in from playing outside, dry your mittens out and use them to create this great book of your very own.

What You Do

1. Fold your sheet of construction paper in half. Place your hand in a mitten and place it on top of the construction paper. Trace around the mitten. Cut out your mitten shape from the folded construction paper to create two mitten cutouts for the front and back covers of your book.

2. Use your mitten shape as a stencil to cut out several mittens from the white paper. Place one of the construction paper mitten shapes in front of your book. Stack the white mitten shapes on top so that the thumbs are lined up. Place the last construction paper mitten on top of the stack.

3. Ask a grown-up to punch two holes in your mitten book on the solid side of your mitten. Thread a piece of yarn through each hole and tie a bow.

4. Decorate the front cover of your mitten book using glitter and markers. Fill your book with winter drawings, poems, stories or photos. Make up a story about your mittens. Mittens are easy to lose. Try making up a story about one of your mittens that has gotten lost. Think about where you may have lost it and what adventure may have occurred.

FROSTY'S WINTER WINDOW WONDERLAND

I or more kids

Even if palm trees are right outside your window this winter, you can look out onto a winter wonderland with these peel-off window decorations you can make yourself.

What You Do

1. Lay newspaper out on your work surface. Draw a great snow picture with your markers on white paper. Be sure to include a snowman and snowflakes in your design.

2. Tape the picture to the newspaper. Place a large piece of wax paper on top of the picture and tape it down to hold it in place. You should be able to see your drawing through the wax paper.

WHAT YOU NEED

Newspaper

Markers

White paper

Tape

Wax paper

3-dimensional fabric paint

Glitter

3. Use the 3-dimensional fabric paint to trace over your picture. Before it dries, you can sprinkle glitter on your design to make it sparkle.

4. Let the paint dry for several hours or overnight. When the paint is thoroughly dry, you will be able to peel it from the wax paper.

5. Decorate a window or your refrigerator with your peel-and-stick snow picture.

SNOWFLAKE MOBILE

I or more kids

It's fun to watch snowflakes fall from the sky on a winter day. They gently land on our hair and clothes. They fall on tree branches, turning them white as if they were spread with white frosting. Think about how the snowflakes look as they fall out of the sky while you create this beautiful mobile of falling snowflakes for your room. The more mobiles you add, the more your room will look like a winter wonderland.

WHAT YOU NEED

I package of white pipe cleaners

Scissors

Beads and glitter (optional)

White thread

Tree branch

❄ A grown-up to help

What You Do

1. Ask a grown-up to cut 3 pipe cleaners in half.

2. Form an X with two of the pipe cleaners and place another in the center to form your basic snowflake shape.

3. Start with the pipe cleaner on the bottom. Take each end of the pipe cleaner and cross on top of the other pipe cleaners. Continue with the other pipe cleaners. This will keep the pipe cleaners in their shape.

4. Fold the extra pipe cleaners that were not used to create the snowflake shape in half and in half again. Cut each fold, creating a number of small pieces.

5. Place two small pipe cleaner pieces on each of the snowflake points by folding them over into a *V* shape. There, you have made a snowflake! Make at least two more for your mobile. If you like, you can string beads or sprinkle glitter on your snowflakes to make them sparkle.

6. Tie a 12- to 16-inch (30 to 40 centimeters) piece of thread to each of the snowflakes and hang from the branch. Attach another thread or yarn to your branch so that you can hang it.

7. Hang your mobile from a ceiling or in a window and watch your room turn into a winter wonderland. Individual snowflakes also look great hanging on a holiday tree. Spread a little winter cheer and mail one to a friend who lives where it doesn't snow.

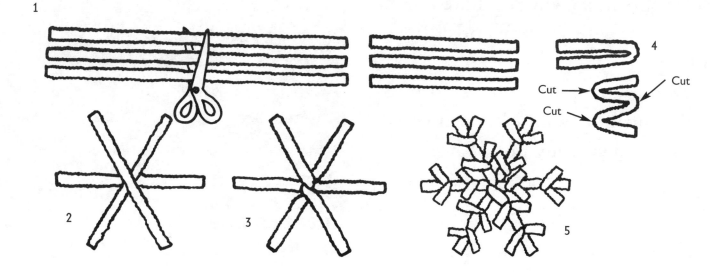

HOT COCOA PARTY

There was a time when tea sets included a pot specifically for hot chocolate. Chocolate bars were not as popular as they are now, and hot chocolate or cocoa was a great way to satisfy a chocolate sweet tooth. It is still a great way to satisfy a sweet tooth, so why not have a hot cocoa party with your friends this winter?

Instant cocoa will always do in a pinch, but here's an old-fashioned recipe for a yummy pot of hot cocoa you may want to try. Ask a grown-up to help you.

Hot Cocoa

I or more kids

WHAT YOU NEED

2 squares good quality chocolate

2 tablespoons (30 ml) sugar

I cup (236 ml) boiling water

3 cups (710 ml) scalded milk (heated to just below the boiling point)

⅛ teaspoon (.6 ml) salt

Whipped cream or marshmallows

Saucepan

Whisk

❄ A grown-up to help

What You Do

1. Ask a grown-up to help with the cooking.

2. Melt the 2 squares of chocolate in a saucepan.

3. Add the sugar and water and let boil for 2 minutes.

4. Add the scalded milk and salt.

5. Whip the chocolate with a whisk. Serve with whipped cream or marshmallows.

Hot Cocoa Party Tips

In England, high tea is served in the afternoon. It is mostly formal. Here are some tips for creating the perfect formal afternoon cocoa party.

1. Dress up for your cocoa party.
2. Set a table with a tablecloth and any fancy plates and cups you can use. Ask a grown-up to help pick out your tableware.
3. Serve yummy finger sandwiches and cookie bars. Since cucumber sand-wiches may not go well with hot cocoa, try date and nut bread with cream cheese or peanut butter and jelly with the crusts cut off.
4. Put on a favorite CD. Classical music is generally played at a high tea, but whatever music is your favorite will make your cocoa party perfect for you.
5. Play games. See who can stack the most cookies or play Marshmallow Mug Toss.

Marshmallow Mug Toss

2 or more kids

Before your mugs are filled with hot cocoa, use them to play this game at your cocoa party.

WHAT YOU NEED

1 mug for each player

10 mini-marshmallows for each player

What You Do

1. Each player stands with a mug directly in front of his feet.

2. Each player takes 10 mini-marshmallows.

3. On the count of three, each player drops his marshmallows, one by one, into his mug while standing upright. The player with the most marshmallows in his mug at the end of the game wins, and can fill his mug with hot chocolate first.

MARSHMALLOW SCULPTURE CONTEST

1 or more kids

The great thing about marshmallow sculptures is that after you're finished making them, you can eat them. You can't do that with a snow sculpture!

What You Do

1. Think of your marshmallows as snowballs. What type of a sculpture would you like to create? You may choose a snowman, an igloo, an animal, or something else.

2. Gather the marshmallows you'll need for your sculpture. Using your fingers, apply the royal icing instead of glue to connect your marshmallows.

3. Set up a contest with your friends. Award prizes for the biggest, the funniest, and the most creative marshmallow sculpture. Can you think of other awards to give out?

Royal Icing

3 egg whites
1/8 teaspoon (.6 ml) cream of tartar
8 ounces (230 g) confectioners' sugar

Whip together the egg whites and cream of tartar until there are soft peaks. Gradually add the confectioners' sugar while stirring.

BUBBLE MAGIC

1 or more kids

Bubbles are a lot of fun to play with in the summer, but did you know that they could be fun to take outside during the winter, too?

What You Do

1. Mix the water, detergent, and glycerin in a bucket.

2. Take the bucket and bubble wand outside on a really cold day, when the thermometer is reading 0 degrees or below.

3. Dip your wand into the bucket and blow gently through the wand to create a bubble. What happened to your bubble? Did it freeze? What happens when you blow your bubbles out into the cold winter wind?

4. Try to keep your bubble on the wand. Allow the bubble to freeze. What happens to the bubble's color when it freezes? Experiment with your bubbles on different days. How does the temperature affect the bubbles?

> ### WHAT YOU NEED
>
> 10 cups (2.3 liters) of water
>
> 1 cup (230 ml) of dishwashing detergent, preferably Joy or Dawn
>
> ¼ cup (59 ml) glycerin (available at natural food and craft stores)
>
> Plastic bucket
>
> Plastic bubble wand

What Is Glycerin?

Glycerin is a clear liquid that has no smell. It is called "hygroscopic," which means that it absorbs water from the air, like a sponge. Natural glycerin is made from oils, like coconut oil. Synthetic glycerin can be made from petroleum. It is used as an ingredient in many things, including soap, candy, and mouth-wash. Look around your house for products that contain glycerin. Hint: Check out toothpastes, syrups, candy, dried fruit, and skin creams. How many items in your home can you find that contain glycerin?

HAWAIIAN LUAU BEACH PARTY

When you are longing for the beach and there is only snow outside, pull out your beach towels and have a Hawaiian Luau Party inside! What do you think you need for a Hawaiian luau? The Hawaiians put together a luau by inviting friends and family, serving great food, playing music, and dancing. That probably sounds like any other party, but add flower leis, hula dancing, and Hawaiian food, and you have an authentic luau.

Flower Leis

1 or more kids

Hawaiian leis are often made with fresh flowers, but not always. Here are directions to make your own flower lei.

WHAT YOU NEED

Colorful paper

Drinking straws

Pipe cleaner

Yarn or ribbon

Scissors

❄ A grown-up to help

What You Do

1. Create paper flowers. Ask a grown-up to help you cut out simple flower shapes about the size of the palm of your hand.

2. Cut the straws into pieces roughly ½ inch (1 centimeter) long.

3. Make a pipe cleaner needle: Fold the pipe cleaner in half. Lay the yarn over the bend in the stem and twist the stem around the yarn.

4. Thread the flowers and straw pieces on the yarn, alternating between the two. Your lei can be worn around your neck, on your wrist or ankle, or around your head.

Hawaiian Luau Party Tips

Here are some other tips for your party.

1. Swing your hips and move your arms from side to side as you try the hula.
2. Enjoy a glass of pineapple juice with a slice of fruit.
3. Can you say "aloha"? Drag out the o to make it even more authentic. That means "hello" in Hawaiian.
4. Find out your name in the Hawaiian language. Go to www.hisurf.com/hawaiian/names.html and type in your English name. Make name tags for your friends with their Hawaiian names.

Puhenehene

4 or more kids

This is a fun game. Translated, it means "finding the pebble."

What You Do

1. Divide the players into two teams.

2. The first team takes the pebble and hides under the blanket, or *kapa* in Hawaiian.

3. The pebble is hidden in a pocket, hand, or sleeve of one of the players under the blanket.

4. When the pebble is hidden, the team uncovers and sits quietly together.

5. The other team looks at the players carefully and tries to figure out who is hiding the pebble. The team is allowed only one guess. If it answers correctly, it gets one point. If it does not answer correctly, the other team gets the point.

6. The teams switch positions and play again. The team that reaches 10 points first wins.

THE GAME OF WINTER

2 or more kids

Have you already played all of your board games and now you're really bored but winter is still around? Well, here's a board game that is as much fun to make as it is to play. It's called the Game of Winter and you get to design it yourself!

What You Do

1. This game is like many board games you have played before. It has a starting point, a path for the players to follow, and a finish; but unlike other games you may have played, in this winter game you get to choose what to include on the board.

2. Place the poster paper on a tabletop. Draw a square in the bottom left-hand corner and mark it the First Day of Winter. Draw another square in the top right-hand corner and mark it the First Day of Spring.

3. Draw a curvy path from one box to the next. Add lines to create boxes along the path.

4. Ask a grown-up to help you write in winter things in your spaces. Think about all the things that have to do with winter. Here are some you can use:

- Build a snowman
- Wake a sleeping bear
- Snow day
- Win a the Iditarod
- Slip on the ice
- Win a sledding race
- Go snowshoeing
- Spy an owl
- Hold a hot cocoa party

5. Add directions to each square, such as "Lose a turn," "Go back 1 space," "Move ahead 2 spaces." For example, if you write "Wake a sleeping bear," you might want to also write "Lose a turn" in that square. If your square reads "Win a sledding race," you might want to add the direction "Move ahead 2 spaces." Don't include a direction in every square.

6. When you have filled in all of your spaces, decorate your game board with pictures.

7. Now you are ready to play. Place your game pieces on the First Day of Winter square. The youngest player goes first. Roll the die and move your button that number of spaces from the starting square. Follow the square directions. The first player to reach the First Day of Spring wins the game!

Board Game Bonanza

Here's an idea for those tired old board games. Plan an afternoon board game swap with your friends. Have them come over with a game that they're a bit tired of playing and a favorite game that you could all play together. Have loads of fun swapping the old games and discovering some new ones, too.

WINTER HOLIDAYS AND FESTIVALS

*Some are old and
some are new,*

*but all should bring much
joy to you.*

TOPSY-TURVY TIME

The winter solstice, the shortest day of the year, marks the beginning of winter and the new solar year. It has long been celebrated throughout the world. The ancient Romans celebrated the winter solstice with a celebration called *Saturnalia*. Like many of our holidays and festivals, the Romans held family dinners and gave gifts. They focused their thoughts on joy, optimism, and goodwill.

Just as we help those around us who are less fortunate during our holidays, the Romans had a similar custom. People traded places with their servants and suspended all the class distinctions that existed. They called it "topsy-turvy time."

Games

Here are some ways to have your own topsy-turvy time just like the ancient Romans.

1. Have a grown-up write a scavenger hunt list, but have them write the words backward! Play Simon Says, but instead of following Simon, reverse the rules. Only do the motions Simon orders without saying Simon Says. For example, if Simon says, "Clap your hands," do it; if Simon says, "Simon says clap your hands," don't do it.

2. Tell knock-knock jokes backward. Tell the answer first and let your friends make up the joke. The best joke wins.

3. Play musical chairs the topsy-turvy way. Sit down when the music plays instead of when it stops.

4. After your games, hold a topsy-turvy banquet. Remember to begin your meal with dessert. Maybe you can begin with upside-down cake!

Pilei

1 or more kids

The ancient Romans, in an effort to be even more informal during Saturnalia, wore paper hats, called *pilei*, to their banquets. Here's how to make your own.

WHAT YOU NEED

Newspaper

Scissors

What You Do

1. Make the newspaper into a square piece of paper. To do this, you must fold one corner down so the bottom edges meet, and cut off the extra strip of paper on the bottom not in the square.

2. Place the paper in front of you. Fold the top of the paper toward you so that the folded paper becomes a triangle.

3. Now fold down the two outer corners so that their sides meet in the middle. You should have another square in front of you.

4. Your square has three layers. Fold the first layer up over the two outside folded triangles. Next, fold the other layer up in the opposite direction. You should have a triangle in front of you. Puff it out to form your hat.

5. Open up the triangle to form your hat. Try it on!

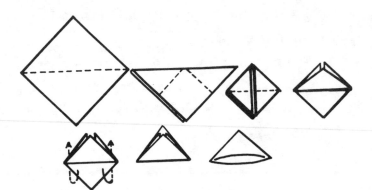

Sigillaria

1 or more kids

No, this is not a new disease. It's the name for small pottery dolls that the Romans gave each other as gifts at the end of Saturnalia. Here's how you can make your own *sigillaria* out of any type of clay to exchange with your friends at your party.

WHAT YOU NEED

Aluminum foil

Air-drying clay or a nontoxic polymer clay from a craft store

Flat work surface

What You Do

1. To create your doll's body, first mold a small piece of aluminum foil into a cone shape. The size depends on how large or small a doll you want to create. Flatten the bottom so that it will stand on its own.

2. Using a flattened hand, roll a piece of clay into a flat sheet to fit over the cone you have already made. Carefully mold the sheet of clay over the cone.

3. To form the head, simply roll the clay into a small ball and stick the ball onto the top of the clay-covered cone.

4. Add arms and feet with other rolled pieces of clay.

5. When your basic doll body is completed, add hair, eyes, and any other features to the doll, using additional pieces of rolled-up clay. Be as creative as you want.

6. Follow the directions on the clay package for drying your doll. Exchange dolls with your friends at the end of your party.

SANTA LUCIA DAY

Santa Lucia Day, a national holiday in Sweden, begins the Christmas season. It is celebrated on December 13 all over Scandinavia and Italy. Lucia was born to a wealthy family in Sicily in the third century. It is said that she carried food to persecuted Christians who were hiding from the Romans in dark tunnels. To light her way, she wore a wreath of candles on her head. She has long been associated with light. Her name, Lucia or Lucy, comes from the word *lux*, meaning light. Her feast day, December 13, was considered the shortest day of the year and people believed Lucia led the way for the longer sun-filled days ahead.

In Sweden, it is traditional for the oldest girl in the family to dress up in a white dress with a red sash and wear a wreath of seven candles on her head. On the morning of December 13, she carries a tray of coffee, buns, and gingersnap cookies to each family member in their room.

Celebrate this holiday of light by making some great beeswax candles and these traditional Santa Lucia cookies.

Beeswax Candles

1 or more kids

You don't have to celebrate Santa Lucia Day to make these great beeswax candles to light up your winter nights.

What You Do

To make a tapered candle:

1. Cut your sheet of beeswax diagonally across.

2. Lay the wax down on the table with the shorter, straight edge to the left. Measure a length of wicking to the length of the left-hand straight side of the wax. Leave the wick just about a half inch longer and cut it.

3. Press the wicking into the edge of the wax, leaving the extra wick at the top. Roll a bit of wax over the wick.

4. Continue rolling the wax tightly to the pointed bottom edge.

5. Press gently to close the edges of your candle. Place your candle in a candlestick and ask a grown-up to light your creation.

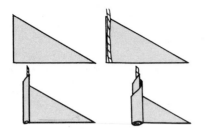

To make a pillar candle:

1. Cut a rectangle shape from your wax the height you would like your candle.

2. Measure the wick, as above, and place it on the short side of the wax.

3. Begin rolling your wax evenly to the end of your sheet. If you would like a thicker candle, add more wax by placing it up against the edge of your candle and pressing the edges together. Continue rolling to your desired thickness.

4. Place your pillar candle on a plate or saucer and enjoy its light for many hours.

Candle Decorations

There are a lot of things you can do to decorate your candles. You easily can add different colored waxes to your pillars and create many different patterns. You can press in small, flattened shapes that you have created from the wax onto your candles to create different themes. Try decorating your candles with stars, hearts, or leaves for a great look. Tie pairs of candles together with a piece of raffia for a great holiday gift.

Gingersnaps (Luciapepparkakor)

1 or more kids

Make these traditional Santa Lucia cookies to share with your family this holiday.

What You Do

1. Place corn syrup, brown sugar, and butter in the saucepan and heat until the butter melts. Put it aside to cool.

2. Mix egg, cloves, ginger, flour (reserve a few tablespoons), and baking soda.

3. Add the syrup and sugar mixture.

4. Place a sheet of wax paper over the bowl and set overnight to let the dough rest.

WHAT YOU NEED

½ cup (120 ml) corn syrup

¾ cup (180 ml) light brown sugar

½ cup (120 ml) butter

Medium saucepan

1 egg

¾ tablespoon (10 ml) cloves

¾ tablespoon (10 ml) ginger

3 cups (700 ml) flour

½ tablespoon (7 ml) baking soda

Large mixing bowl

Wax paper

Rolling pin

Cookie cutters

Baking sheet

½ cup (120 ml) confectioners' sugar

½ egg white

Icing bag

❋ A grown-up to help

5. Sprinkle the reserved flour on to the work surface. Place the dough in the center of the surface and, using the rolling pin, roll the dough until it is a thin sheet.

6. Using the cookie cutters, cut out cookie shapes. Place the cookies on a greased cookie sheet.

7. Ask a grown-up to help with the oven. Bake at 350° F (175° C) for about 6 minutes. Leave the cookies on the cookie sheet to cool. Cooled cookies can be decorated with royal icing (see page 103 for the recipe).

HAPPY CHINESE NEW YEAR

I or more kids

Even if you have already celebrated the New Year on January 1, here's your chance to celebrate it again, the Chinese way. The Chinese New Year, or Spring Festival, does not fall on January 1 because the Chinese calendar is a combination of the 12-month calendar and a lunar-solar calendar system. Instead, the Chinese New Year falls somewhere between late January and mid-February. After a few days, the festival is concluded with the beautiful Lantern Festival.

Here are some activities to make your celebration of the Chinese New Year extra special.

Paper Lanterns

An old legend tells of a village in China that was attacked by a monster on a cold winter night.

The monster attacked the same village at the same time the following year. The villagers decided that they needed to scare the monster away so that it would not attack them again. The following year the villagers hung red banners, because it is believed that the color red keeps away evil. Along with the bright red banners, the villagers set off loud, beautiful fireworks and banged on drums to keep the monster away. Thankfully, their plan worked and they celebrated for several days.

During the Chinese New Year, people still decorate with a lot of red. They paint doors and windows with fresh coats of red paint. They hang paper decorations that are decorated with the Chinese characters that represent wealth, happiness, and good fortune, and they hang beautiful lanterns. Make this paper lantern to celebrate the New Year in your home.

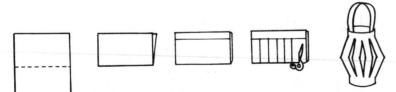

WHAT YOU NEED

Red paper, 8½ × 11 inches (28 × 28 cm) or larger

Glue

Glitter, markers, or paints for decoration

Scissors

Ruler

What You Do

1. If you would like an overall pattern on your lantern, decorate your paper before you begin the other steps.

2. Fold the paper in half.

3. Measure a line two inches from the open end of the fold and draw a thin line with a pencil.

4. Starting at the folded edge, cut along strips to the line you have marked all along the fold.

5. Unfold your paper and apply glue along the side. Join the two ends together to form your lantern.

6. Cut a thin strip of paper. Apply glue to each end of the strip. Decide which end of your lantern will be the top and glue in the strip of paper to form a handle. You can hang your lantern just the way it is for a great Chinese New Year decoration or dim the lights and hold a flashlight inside for a wonderful glow.

More Ways to Celebrate the Chinese New Year

The celebration lasts for 15 days and each day has a special meaning. For example, the second day is believed to be the birthday of all dogs. Celebrants feed and treat their dogs especially well on this day. Here are some ideas to increase your fun:

- Oranges and tangerines symbolize good fortune. Share one with a friend.
- It's a tradition for spring cleaning to be completed by the new year. See if you can help with your family's spring cleaning.
- Wish someone prosperity and wealth with the Chinese words *Gung Hey Fat Choy.*

Hot Spiced Cider—A Favorite New Year Drink

1 or more kids

What You Do

1. Pour 8 cups (1.9 liters) of apple cider in a saucepan.

2. Add several orange or lemon slices, 2 cinnamon sticks, and 4 cloves.

3. Ask a grown-up for help with the stove. Simmer on low until warm and pour into mugs.

WHAT YOU NEED

8 cups (1.9 liters) apple cider

Saucepan

Orange or lemon slices

2 cinnamon sticks

4 cloves

❄ A grown-up to help

Rain Water, Pure Brightness, and Other Times of the Year

The Chinese calendar is divided by 24 terms that describe changes in nature. Some of the terms include Spring Equinox, Great Heat, Cold Dew, and Great Snow. Can you tell by the term Waking of Insects when it might fall in the Chinese calendar? If you guessed March, you would be right!

This Is the Animal That Hides in Your Heart

Do you know your zodiac sign? It might be Aquarius, Taurus, Cancer, or another sign. Your zodiac sign is determined by the date and month you are born. Chinese zodiac signs are determined by the year you are born. They are all named after animals. The Chinese New Year marks the beginning of a new zodiac sign. It cycles every 12 years. To find your Chinese sign, look on the chart below to find the year you were born.

Chinese Signs

- Horse 1990, 2002
- Sheep 1991, 2003
- Monkey 1992, 2004
- Rooster 1993, 2005
- Dog 1994, 2006
- Boar 1995, 2007

- Rat 1996, 2008
- Ox 1997, 2009
- Tiger 1998, 2010
- Rabbit 1999, 2011
- Dragon 2000, 2012
- Snake 2001, 2013

GROUNDHOG DAY SHADOW TAG

2 or more kids

Every year on February 2, people all around the country wait to hear Punxsutawney Phil's weather prediction. Punxsutawney Phil is not your average weather forecaster. You see, Punxsutawney Phil is a groundhog. Is it true? Can Punxsutawney Phil really tell us whether or not there will be six more weeks of winter just by seeing his shadow (or not) on February 2?

If the groundhog has seen his shadow and the sun is shining, head outdoors with a friend to play shadow tag.

What You Do

The object of shadow tag is not to tag your friend but to tag your friend's shadow. At the same time that you are trying to step on your friend's shadow, your friend is trying to step on your shadow. The more friends and the more room you have to play, the more fun you'll have. If you can avoid being tagged, you become the winner.

Weather Sayings

There are many weather sayings you might have heard. Here are just a couple:

The larger the dark bands on a woolly bear caterpillar, the more severe the winter.

Wet May, dry July.

*As high as the weeds grow
So will be the bank of snow.*

Try making up your own weather saying.

NEW YEAR'S EVE SCRAPBOOK

1 or more kids

This may not be the start of a new millennium, but it is still a great time to look toward the future. So, while you are making New Year's resolutions, take some time to think about who you are and what you will be like in the future. Then, make a scrapbook that tells all about you. It will be a lot of fun to look at the pages you've created next year and the years after!

What You Do

1. Gather all of the items that you want to include in your scrapbook. Read the planning tips below to help you decide what items you want to include.

2. Pick a page to begin your scrapbook, for example, All About Me or My Family.

3. Select the paper that you want to be the background page color. Choose one or more colors that work well with that paper color.

4. Arrange your pictures on the page. Ask a grown-up to help you cut the coordinating paper into frames or mats for your pictures. The easy way to do this is to glue your pictures on the paper you would like to be the frame and then cut around each picture, leaving a border of the paper.

5. Using your glue stick, attach your framed pictures to your page.

6. Let your page tell a story. Start with a title. Write down anything that your pictures leave out. For example, label the pictures with names, dates, and location. Include things that tell more about the subject. If the page is about your family, you might want to write something special about each member of your family with their picture.

7. When you have finished each page of your scrapbook, use the three-hole punch or place each page in a page protector before placing it in the binder.

Be sure to place your completed scrapbook in a safe spot so that next year you can pull it out on New Year's Eve. You might even start a tradition of adding one page each year to your book. Imagine what it would look like 10 years from now!

Planning Tips for Making Your New Year's Eve Scrapbook

1. Think about yourself. What is your favorite game, food, and color? What makes you different from everyone else? When you are planning your scrapbook, you need to think about what things you can add to it that will tell someone who opens it years from now who you were when you created it—even if that person that opens it is you!

2. It is great to include a picture of yourself in your scrapbook, but it is also fun to draw a picture of yourself and your family and include that with it. Use the acid-free paper for your drawing. You can also include a drawing or photo of your house.

3. Write a letter to the future you. What would you tell yourself in 10 years? Would you tell yourself all about who you are now or would you tell yourself what you hope you are like in the future?

4. Write down your predictions for the future. What are some things that you think might happen to your school, your family, our world?

5. Include a picture of your favorite toys. Perhaps you love yo-yos, trading cards, dolls, or beanbag toys. Don't forget to also include a picture of your room.

MARTINMAS

I or more kids

Many, many years ago there lived a man named Martin. He was a Roman soldier who rode a noble horse and wore a regal cloak that kept the harsh winds off his body.

One day as he was riding with the army he saw a beggar. This man had little on his back to keep him warm, and Martin saw how cold he was. Out of the goodness in his heart, Martin took his sword and sliced his cloak in two, giving the beggar half of the cloak to keep himself warm.

That was centuries ago, but people still remember the kindness that Martin showed to the beggar. On November 11, many Europeans celebrate Martin's kindness in a holiday called "Martinmas." Children lead a procession with lanterns and songs are sung. You can celebrate the holiday by acting with the same kindness as Martin. Here are some ideas of things that you can do in your community.

What You Do

- Go through your closet and room to find clothes, toys, and books that you have outgrown. Box them up for a local charity.

- Adopt a senior citizen. Visit and help them with their daily chores.

- Collect books to donate to your library.

- Visit a local nursing home and sing songs to the residents.

- Gather up canned food items from neighbors to bring to the local food pantry.

- Make a welcome box to give to a new student in your school. Include a map of your town, the best places to buy ice cream and pizza, information on favorite parks, and some school supplies to start them off.

WINTER OLYMPICS

Go for the silver, bronze, or gold.

There's so much fun to behold.

133

BROOMBALL

4 or more kids

roomball is very similar to hockey. It is played by kids in many different countries, including Canada and Australia. In this version, a snow-covered driveway replaces the ice where it is normally played.

What You Do

1. Ask a grown-up to help you shovel the driveway to make it smooth for your game.

2. Set up your goalposts about three feet apart on either end of the playing area or court. Make sure your court is in a safe area, away from any cars or traffic.

3. Players divide into two equal teams. Each team should have at least two players. Each team should face its opponent's goal.

4. The object of broomball is to shoot the ball through your opponent's goalposts. Ask a grown-up to set the ball in play by tossing it into the center of the court. Use the end of the broom to push the ball across the court and into the goal. You may want to practice passing the ball back and forth to your teammates before you start an actual game.

5. The winning team is the team that scores the most goals.

Broomball History in the United States

Broomball leagues sprang up in Minnesota back in 1961. The first team was based in Minneapolis. In 1994 the United States Broomball Association was formed. Today, broomball is played in many states across the United States. Someday we may see this played in the Olympics right along with hockey.

TRACK AND SNOW

2 or more kids

Running and jumping hurdles is a fun Olympic sport to watch in the summer. Here's a great way to enjoy it this winter.

What You Do

1. Ask a grown-up to shovel a path of snow across a lawn or grassy area, leaving three snow piles along the path, each about two feet or so high.

2. See if you can jump over the snow pile. If it is too low, add a little more snow. If it is a bit too high, take off some.

3. Plan some races over the snow pile hurdles with your friends. See who can jump the farthest, quickest, and finish the races first.

OLYMPIC SNOWBALL

4 or more kids

Kids in Greece know this game as Olympic ball and play it in warm weather. Here is a winter version of this game from the home of the Olympics.

What You Do

1. Players divide into two teams. Each team forms two lines facing each other.

2. Each team takes a snowball and begins to throw the snowball back and forth between the two lines of the same team.

3. If one team drops its snowball, the other team is awarded 5 points. The first team to reach 50 points wins.

WHAT YOU NEED

Snowballs

CRAZY SLED RACE

2 or more kids

ear the site of the 1932 and 1980 Winter Olympics in Lake Placid is a small village called Bolton Landing. Every year, Bolton Landing has a bed race. Contestants decorate beds, put them on wheels, and race them down the main street in the village. Can you imagine all of those beds rolling down the street? Well, here is your chance to try something similar, but using sleds instead of beds!

What You Do

1. Ask all of your friends to bring over their sleds to decorate. Tie on streamers, bells, and any other crafty thing you can think of to decorate your sled. Give your sled a name or a number, and fly a banner or flag off the back of it. Ask a grown-up to check them over to make sure that your decorations do not hamper the mobility of your sled.

2. Take your sleds to a nearby hillside or sledding course. You might have to use a spare sled to make your own course if there isn't one already there. Make sure that the sledding course will accommodate all of your sleds.

3. Invite neighbors, friends, and parents to watch your race. Line up all of your sleds

and, on the count of three, take off down the course.

4. Have your spectators give out the ribbons for the sleds that are the fastest, funniest, prettiest, craziest, and so on. Don't forget to have someone take pictures of your crazy sleds.

Award Badges

What You Do

1. Ask a grown-up to help you cut out several circles of the fun foam. Each circle should be roughly three inches in diameter.

2. Using the markers, decorate the fun foam circles with the award description. You may want to draw a silly face on the award for the silliest or a shooting star for the fastest.

3. Turn the badges over and glue the pin backs to the other side of each badge.

MAKE A FIGURE EIGHT

1 or more kids

Early skaters were not given points for their jumps and spins like the Olympic skaters you see today. Instead, it was the marks that they left on the surface of the ice that made them champions. Early competitions in figure skating were based on 41 figures that were derived from the basic figure eight. Skaters competed in creating these figures on the ice surface. In fact, that is how figure skating got its name! See what figures you can create on the surface of the ice after you strap on a pair of skates and learn how to make a classic figure eight on the ice.

What You Do

1. Imagine a figure eight on the ice before you. Stand in the position where the two circles would intersect.

2. Place your feet at right angles, with the heel of the right foot touching the instep of the left foot. Push off with the left foot. Try to skate like a champion figure skater and not let the other foot touch the ice as you form a circle, returning to the spot where you started.

3. Continue skating past the spot where you started, switch feet, and begin skating the second circle of the figure eight.

4. Return again to where you started your figure eight. Hurrah, you did it!

Skating History

Proof of early skaters became evident when a skeleton dating back from 10,000 B.C. was found in the peat bogs of the Netherlands with animal bone blades tied to his feet. Around 1000 A.D. skating had entered Scandinavia as a means of transportation, and by the early 15th century speed races had begun to spring up in European towns. By the time the first Winter Olympics were held in 1924, skating had already appeared at the Summer Games in 1908 and 1920. Skating was here to stay.

CURLING

4 or more kids

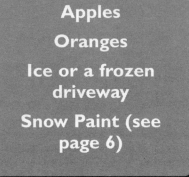

WHAT YOU NEED

Apples

Oranges

Ice or a frozen driveway

Snow Paint (see page 6)

Curling made a successful debut at the 1998 Winter Olympics in Nagano, Japan. Since then, it has become even more popular around the world. Curling is a little like bowling, a little like shuffleboard, and a little like bocce. The game is played with stones, which are moved on ice in a manner similar to bowling. Two teams try to move their stones closest to the center of the ice, using brooms to sweep the ice, while moving their opponents away from the center.

Here is a variation of this new Olympic sport that replaces the large, heavy stone with some fruit you may have around your house this winter.

What You Do

1. Divide into two teams. Each player on the first team takes an apple and each player on the second team takes an orange.

2. Find the center of your playing area. You want to roll the apple or orange to the center of the ice, which is called the house. Mark the house in your playing area with some snow paint (see page 6).

3. The apple team goes first. Each player, in turn, takes an apple and rolls it toward the house. The orange team then rolls its oranges.

4. Only one team scores during each end (inning). The number of points scored is the total number of one team's stones (fruit) that are closer to the house than the closest of the opponent's stones (fruit).

Curling History

Some say that curling was invented by the English. Others say it was invented in Scotland. Its true origins are murky, but it was the Scottish people who had the most influence on the game during the past 500 years. Originally it was played on frozen ponds and streams, but now it's mostly played indoors during the winter months by clubs all over the world.

5. Curling has a total of eight ends. At the end of the eight ends, the team with the highest score wins.

SNOWBALL SHOT PUT

2 or more kids

The Olympic shot put event dates back to the first modern Olympics in 1896. The shot is actually a heavy iron or brass ball that is "put" or thrown off the shoulder of the thrower. Try it this winter with a snowball and see how far you can throw it shot-put style.

What You Do

1. Place the snowball in your hand.

2. Bend your arm at your elbow and hold your hand with your palm facing upward. Your hand should be positioned near your chin.

3. Extend your arm straight out in front of you to push, or "put" the snowball into the air. Where did it land? Try it again and see if you can put it farther than the first time. Have a contest with your friends to see who can throw a snowball the farthest, shot-put style.

FAVORITE WINTER BOOKS, VIDEOS, AND WEB SITES

Into the Snow!

Books

Andersen, Hans Christian. *The Snow Queen*. Cambridge, MA: Candlewick Press, 1996.

Croll, Carolyn. *The Little Snowgirl: An Old Russian Tale*. New York: Putnam Publishing Group, 1989.

Guinness World Record Editors. *Guinness Book of World Records*. New York: Bantam Books, 2000. (Look for the snow angel record.)

Martin, Jacqueline Briggs. *Snowflake Bentley*. Boston, MA: Houghton Mifflin Company, 1998.

Videos

The Snow Queen, produced by Faerie Tale Theater. 1983.

The Snowman, Raymond Briggs. Columbia Tristar, 1982.

Web Sites

Kamakura Festival **www.media-akita.or.jp/akita-events/kamakura2E.html**

Snowshoeing **www.svidaho.com/snowshoeing**

Fun and Games

Books

Van Stockum, Hilda. *A Day on Skates: The Story of a Dutch Picnic*. Vancouver, British Columbia, Canada: Bethlehem Books, 1997.

Winter Critters

Books

Benjamin, Cynthia. *Footprints in the Snow*. New York: Scholastic, 1994.

Boyle, Doe. *Summer Coat, Winter Coat: The Story of a Snowshoe Hare*. Norwalk, CT: Soundprints Corp., 1995.

Carlstrom, Nancy White. *Midnight Dance of the Snowshoe Hare: Poems of Alaska*. New York: Philomel Books, 1998.

Rey, H. A. *Find the Constellations*. New York: Houghton Mifflin Co., 1976.

Yolen, Jane. *Owl Moon*. New York: Putnam Publishing Group, 1987.

Arctic Adventures

Books

Dwyer, Mindy. *Aurora: A Tale of the Northern Lights*. Anchorage, AK: Alaska Northwest Books, 1997.

Kinsey-Warnock, Natalie. *The Fiddler of the Northern Lights*. New York: Dutton Children's Books, 1996.

Lewin, Ted. *The Reindeer People*. New York: Simon & Schuster, 1994.

Parkison, Jami. *Inger's Promise*. Kansas City, MO: Marsh Media, 1995.

Sierra, Judy. *Antarctic Antics: A Book of Penguin Poems*. San Diego, CA: Harcourt Brace, 1998.

Standiford, Natalie. *The Bravest Dog Ever: The True Story of Balto*. New York: Random House, 1989.

Videos

Balto, MCA Home Video, 1996.

Prancer, MGM, 1999.

Rudolph the Red-Nosed Reindeer, Sony, 1964.

Web Sites

New England Aquarium's *Be a Penguin!*
www.neaq.org

Soapstone artists in Sanikiluaq, Nanuvut
www.soapstoneartists.com

Cabin Fever

Books

Brett, Jan. *The Mitten*. New York: Putnam Publishing Group, 1996.

Hader, Berta. *Big Snow*. New York: Aladdin Books, 1988.

Web Sites

Bubbles
www.exploratorium.edu/ronh/bubbles
and http://bubbles.org

Hawaiian names
www.hisurf.com/hawaiian/names.html

Jan Brett   www.janbrett.com

Snowdomes
www.snowdomes.com and
www.beckleycardy.com/~wenlinh/whatsha
kin.html

Winter Holidays and Festivals

Books

Jackson, Ellen. *The Winter Solstice*. Brookfield, CT: Millbrook Press, 1997.

Web Sites

Learn the Santa Lucia songs in Italian and Swedish at
www.serve.com/shea/germusa.lucylied.htm

Winter Olympics

Books

Brimner, Larry D. *The Winter Olympics*. New York: Children's Press, 1997.

Koda-Callan, Elizabeth. *The Shiny Skates*. New York: Workman Publishing Co., 1992.

Krementz, Jill. *A Very Young Skater*. New York: Alfred A. Knopf, 1979.

O'Connor, Jane. *Kate Skates*. New York: Putnam Publishing Group, 1995.

Videos

The Ice Princess. Winstar, 1998. This video stars Katarina Witt.

Web Sites

Broomball
http://efn.org/~msayer/usba/index.shtml

Curling
http://cbs.sportsline.com/u/olympics/nagano98/features/kidzone/kid_curling.html

History of figure skating
www.skatinghistory.com

Information on your favorite figure skater
www.usfsa.org

WINTER FESTIVALS AND CARNIVALS

UNITED STATES

Alaska

Anchorage

Fur Rendezvous

Every February
Information: (907) 274-1177 or
www.furrondy.net

The biggest winter festival in Alaska. This is a great way to sample all of the winter activities in Anchorage. Nine days of fireworks, snowshoe softball games, Eskimo blanket tosses, fireworks, jazz, film festival, stage shows, and more.

Willow

Willow Winter Carnival

Every January
Information: (907) 495-6633

Dogsled racing, snow-machine racing, x-country ski event, and talent show are included among the festivities here.

Arizona

Flagstaff

Winterfest

**Held annually throughout February
Information: (800) 842-7293 or
www.flagstaffarizona.org**

Concerts, sled dog racing, cross country
skiing, and a host of other activities
throughout the month of February highlight
this annual event.

California

Kingsburg

**Held second Saturday in December
Information: (559) 897-1111**

If you are near Fresno, California, stop by
the Swedish village of Kingsburg, about a half
hour drive southeast of Fresno, for a great day
of **Santa Lucia** activities. The festival includes
an evening parade, Swedish baked goods, and
arts and crafts. If you arrive early enough in the
morning, duck into a village restaurant for
breakfast and a chance to see a traditional Santa
Lucia procession. You will even hear the song
"Santa Lucia" sung in Swedish.

Colorado

Aspen

Winterskol

**Held annually in January or February
Information: Aspen Chamber Resort
Association (970) 925-1940**

Visitors to Aspen, Colorado can take some time
away from the ski slopes to enjoy **Winterskol**, an
annual festival that has been celebrated for
about 50 years.

Connecticut

Stamford

Winterfest

**Third Sunday in January
Information: (203) 322-1646**

Visit with reindeer, learn about ice harvesting, enjoy horse-drawn hayrides and many other winter events at this great winterfest.

Florida

Fort Lauderdale

Winterfest

**Second or third Saturday in December
Information: (954) 767-0686 or
www.winterfestparade.com**

The lighted Boat Parade is the highlight of this winterfest, but there are many other activities throughout the month of December to check out.

Idaho

McCall

Winter Carnival

**Date and Event Information:
(888) 844-3246 or
www. inidaho.com/wintercarn.htm**

Check out this great winter carnival, which has been celebrated in Idaho for over 30 years. You'll find many spectacular snow sculptures, dog sled races, tubing, skiing, and many other activities for the whole family to enjoy. Enter the Kids' Snowman Building Contest and test out those skills you've been honing during the winter.

Iowa

Decorah

Barnelopet

**First Saturday in February
Information: (319) 382-9681**

Vesterheim Norwegian-American Museum and the Sons of Norway sponsor this annual event. It is a noncompetitive 2.5K cross-country or walking race for kids ages 3 to 13. The small entry fee includes bib and medal. Participants can enjoy hot cocoa and cookies, too.

Maine

Medawaska

International Snowmobilers Festival

First weekend in February
Information: (207) 728-7000

Even if you don't snowmobile, check out this festival in Maine. You'll love the fireworks.

Maryland

Ocean City

Ocean City Winterfest

November through the rest of the winter
Information: (800) oc-ocean or
www.ococean.com

Tree lighting in mid-November, followed by thousands of lights lighting up Northside Park through the beginning of January. Visit at dusk for a train ride through the park.

Massachusetts

Boston

First Night

December 31
Information:
(617) 357-0065 or
http://firstnightintl.org/cities.cfm

Celebrate First Night in Boston or in a community near you. First Night is a great way for families to celebrate New Year's Eve. Founded in Boston in 1976 as a finale to the city's Bicentennial celebration, First Night has now spread to over 200 other locations. These community celebrations throughout the United States and other countries celebrate the New Year through the arts with parades, music, and family activities.

Michigan

Holland

Dutch WinterFest

Begins the first Friday in December and continues during the month
Information: (800) 506-1299

Go Dutch and visit the town with heated sidewalks and a great winter festival.

Sinterklaas, a Dutch incarnation of Santa Claus, rides into town on a white horse. Street musicians play, too.

Plymouth

Plymouth International Ice Sculpture Spectacular

Held annually in January
Information: 44833 N. Territorial Road, Plymouth, MI 48170; (713) 459-6969; or www.oeonline.com/plymouthice/

For more than 15 years, Plymouth, Michigan, has hosted the Plymouth International Ice Sculpture Spectacular, with carvers visiting from all over the world. It is the largest and oldest ice sculpture event in the country. Talk about inspiration!

Minnesota

Minneapolis

Santa Lucia Celebrations

Held annually on the Sunday closest to December 13
Information and ticket sales:
(612) 871-4907

There are Santa Lucia celebrations all over Minnesota. Among the celebrations in Minneapolis is the event sponsored by the American-Swedish Institute. Their procession not only includes Santa Lucia, but her attendants, star boys, and gnomes. Gingersnaps and Santa Lucia buns are served to ticket holders.

St. Paul

St. Paul Winter Carnival

Information: (800) 488-4023

The St. Paul Winter Carnival in Minnesota is one of the greatest winter festivals in the world.

It was begun in 1886, after the city was called the "Siberia of North America." To prove that winter was a season to celebrate, the people of St. Paul took action and created a festival that not only boasts great ice sculptures, but fireworks, parades, and ice skating, as well.

New Hampshire

Lincoln

Winterfest

Octagon Base Area at Loon Mountain
Times vary each year
Information: (603) 745-8111

Visitors to the New Hampshire's White Mountains can spend time away from the slopes to enjoy fondue parties, marshmallow roasting, pond skating, and a great cross-country torchlight parade through the valley.

New Mexico

Fort Sumner

Fort Sumner Winterfest

Held the second Saturday in December
Information: (505) 355-7705

Giant Christmas cards and over 800 luminaries decorate the historic streets of Fort Sumner for the Winterfest.

New York

Lake George

Lake George Winter Carnival

Throughout February
Information: Lake George Chamber of Commerce: (518) 668-5755, or Warren County Tourism office: (518) 761-6366

The Lake George Winter Carnival has been a long-standing tradition in this Adirondack town. It runs the entire month of February with all kinds of activities, including a polar club swim, children's fair, ice sculpture contests, and more.

North Carolina

Blowing Rock

Blowing Rock Winterfest

In mid-January
Information: (888) 465-0366 or
www.blowingrockwinterfest.com

A great three-day festival of music including bluegrass and folk, puppet shows, and other activities.

North Dakota

Devil's Lake

Shiverfest

One weekend in February
Information: (701) 662-4903

This looks like a new annual event for North Dakota. The February weekend fest includes a treasure hunt, sled dog races, kids' fishing tournament, and a beard-growing competition.

Ohio

Mansfield

Winter Ski Carnival

Third or fourth week in February
Information: (419) 774-9818

Snowboard races and other fun for families during this festival that has been taking place for more than 40 years.

Oklahoma

Watonga

Native Winterfest

January
Information: (800) 892-8690

Includes soap making, native foods, lotion and potion making, and other indoor activities at the Lodge and Nature Center of the Roman Nose State Park. Park officials are looking forward to making this an annual event.

Rhode Island

Newport

Winter Festival

February
Information: (800) 976-5122,
www.newportevents.com, or
www.gonewport.com

Take a break from touring the spectacular mansions to enjoy the citywide scavenger hunt, ice sculptures, and fantasy auction. Family Day at Easton's Beach, complete with a sand sculpture contest, is an event not to miss.

South Dakota

Aberdeen

Winter Carnival

First weekend in February
Information: (605) 225-5325

Call for more information on this carnival, which includes bobsled races and ice-skating.

Lead

Winterfest

Every January
Information: (605) 584-1100

This two-day event includes a parade, children's carnival, sled races, and a snowman-making contest.

Tennessee

Pigeon Forge and Gatlinburg

Smoky Mountain Winterfest

Throughout the winter
Information: Gatlinburg: (800) 952-8743 and Pigeon Forge: (800) 251-9100 or www.thewebstation.com/winterfest/

If you are planning a visit to Dollywood this winter, you'll have a chance to take in some of the planned winterfest events. Take a peek at the events calendar to see when the Wilderness Wildlife Week of Nature is planned for many free outdoor activities for the whole family to enjoy.

Vermont

Stowe

Stowe Winter Carnival

Information: (800) 247-8693 or
www.stowewintercarnival.com

Winter carnivals have been held in New England for over a century, and Vermont still hosts many throughout the state. The largest events are held in Stowe and Mad River Valley. Since 1921, Stowe has featured great events at their winter carnival, like the World's Coldest Parade, Snow Golf, Snow Volleyball, ski jumping, and youth hockey.

Mad River Valley

Winter Festival of Events

Throughout winter
Information: (800) 82-VISIT

Mad River Valley has stretched out their winter carnival to last all winter. It's now called the Winter Festival of Events and features many family activities, especially during the February school break and Christmas week.

Wisconsin

Madison

Kites on Ice

Information: www.madfest.org/kites.htm

If you thought flying kites was an activity for a summer day, think again. Kites on Ice, first held in 1999, brings this summer pastime to new heights—literally. Join kite enthusiasts from England, Germany, France, Canada, and the United States for a spectacular festival full of color and magic on the ice in Madison.

CANADA
Alberta

Calgary

Calgary Winterfest

**Held annually for 11 days in February
Information: (877) 543-5480 or
www.calgarywinterfest.com/**

Carnival entertainment, curling competitions, wacky wing-eating contest, ice sculpting and a lot of other fun activities.

Ontario

BonSoo

**February
Information: www.bonsoo.con.ca**

For more than 38 years, this festival has delighted visitors for 10 days in February. It offers more than 100 indoor and outdoor activities, including curling, fireworks, snow sculpting, dog pulling, snowshoeing, snowman storytime, and a lot of great music.

Niagara Falls

Winter Festival of Lights

**Held November through January
Information: (905) 374-1616,
(800) 56-FALLS (32557), or
www.niagarafallstourism.com/wfol/wfol
main.html**

More than 50 wonderful light displays, including a Disney motion light display. Visit early in January and you might be able to catch the light display on the New York side as well. The festival includes parades, fireworks, music, and more.

Ottawa

Winterlude

**Three weekends in February
Information: (800) 465-1867**

Canada's capital city really knows how to throw a great winter festival. Every two years special activities are planned to celebrate their ties with Australia, but even if you come on an off year there are some great annual events, including sledge hockey, winter camping, snowshoe races, and hot air balloons. A favorite among visitors is the snow cinema set up on a huge snow screen.

Quebec

Winter Carnival

**17 days in February
Information: www.carnaval.qc.cc**

This event began back in 1894, but has been an official annual event since 1955. Stretched out over 17 days in February are all sorts of winter festivities, presided over by a jolly snowman named Bonhomme Carnaval. Favorites each year are the igloo village, where visitors can take workshops in igloo building and even spend the night, and Bonhomme's castle of snow.

There are many other winterfests held each year throughout the world. To find one near you, visit **www.festivals.com** or contact your local tourism office.

About the Author

Nancy F. Castaldo is the author of *The Little Hands Nature Book*, recipient of the 1996 Parent's Choice Doing and Learning Approval, and *Rainy Day Play!*, an American Bookseller's Pick of the Lists.

A native of New York's Hudson Valley, she earned a Bachelor of Science degree from Marymount College and a Master of Arts from the State University of New York. She is a Girl Scout leader and member of the Board of Directors for her local Girl Scout council. As an environmental educator, author, and Girl Scout volunteer, she has led numerous children's workshops. She lives in upstate New York with her husband, daughter, dog, cat, and an occasional turtle. Check out her web site at www.nancycastaldo.com to learn more about Nancy and her books.